OF LIFE AND AUTOMOBILES

STORIES OF ENTHUSIASTS & THEIR BONDS WITH THEIR CARS

FRANK ADKINS

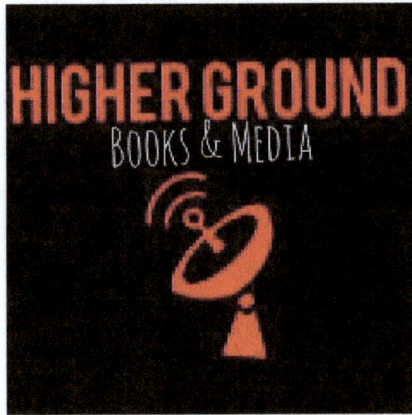

Higher Ground Books & Media
Springfield, Ohio.
http://highergroundbooksandmedia.com

Cover photos by: Joe Cann, Top Photo
                 Jenni Romano, Bottom Photo

Printed in the United States of America 2022

OF LIFE AND AUTOMOBILES

STORIES OF ENTHUSIASTS &
THEIR BONDS WITH THEIR CARS

FRANK ADKINS

Dedication

Dedicated to the memories of my father, Frank Adkins Sr., my uncle, Richard Adkins Sr., and my grandfather, William Adkins.

Foreword

When I was younger, I went to car shows and cruises to see the cool cars. No matter if it was the fifticth time I looked at a particular car, I'd scrutinize it as if I were seeing it for the first time. Now when I go to a car show, I park with friends. We pull our chairs together in the shade, and we catch up on the happenings in each other's lives. Often, other show participants have begun leaving before I even start to peruse the field of cars. And that is just fine with me.

I have realized that the car hobby is as much about the people as it is the cars. The cars bring us together, but the friendships and camaraderie keep us involved. Most of my friendships have been forged through my connections with automobiles, and I am reminded of that every year when I look at our Christmas card list. Some of those friendships have endured for decades.

It was the muscle cars of the '60s and '70s that drew me into this hobby, and those are the cars that I'm the most enthusiastic about today. Now that the cars of that era are half a century old, few remain with their original owners. Many of these cars have colorful histories, but it is impossible to tell the stories of our cars without also telling the stories of their owners, the people who drove them, and/or the folks who worked on them. Our stories are so intertwined that it is often impossible to separate the two. This realization has fueled many of the stories I have written for Cruising Magazine (cruisingmagazine.net) over the last seventeen seasons. In fact, I am sharing a few of those stories here.

In selecting the stories for this book, my goal was to choose those that not only involved cars, but that had at least an equally strong human content. We may be car junkies to the end, but we are, first and foremost, human.

Although I had considered writing a book such as this from time to time over the years, it was Rebecca Benston, the CEO of Higher Ground Books and Media, who gave me the nudge that set things in motion. The older I get, the more I marvel at the mysterious ways in which God works. I was facing shoulder surgery, and I knew I would be some time before I would be able to work on the small fleet of old cars that my wife, Kristan, and I own. To keep myself from going stir crazy while recuperating during the long, gray winter months, I needed a project. I had a few book ideas, but none of them ignited a fire in my belly. Rebecca's perfectly timed suggestion did just that.

Writers find inspiration in the strangest places, but the people in our lives motivate us and support us throughout the writing process. Nobody has ever pushed or supported me more than my wife, Kristan. To her I say thank you for seeing me through yet another book, for being my sounding board, and for helping me come up with titles (something I stink at!) Of course, I owe a huge debt of gratitude to Rebecca Benston, for without her timely suggestion, the idea for this book would still be rolling around in the back of my head. I'd like to express my gratitude to Jerry DuPhily, the CEO of TSN Publishing in Wilmington, Delaware, which produces and distributes Cruising Magazine. Jerry has always been supportive of his staff, and he has given me his blessing in sharing some of my stories from the back issues of Cruising in this book.

I want to thank Greg Rager, Rita Shaw, Randy Lowe, Steve Gray, Mark and Pam Shane, Susan Stanley, Bryan and Heather Rash, Adrianna Straub, Bill and Leta Berry, Amy Bragg, Scott and Felicia Smith, Jenni Romano, Rob McCall, and Kevin Pampuch. Not only did these folks share their stories with me, they allowed me to tell their stories to everyone who reads this book. I am honored that they put their trust in me, and I hope I haven't let them down.

Finally, I would be remiss if I didn't thank you, my dear reader. I am grateful to you for plunking down the cash to obtain a copy of this book, but it means even more to me that you are willing invest your time to read it. It is my sincerest hope that you enjoy it.

-Frank

A Brush with Royalty

Through years of participation in various auto-related events, I have met several famous people including Richard Petty, Herb McCandless, Ronnie Sox, Vincent D'Onofrio, Linda Vaughn, Bill "Maverick" Golden, and Dennis Gage. In the late 1990s, due to our competing in One Lap of America (which rose from the ashes of the Cannonball Baker Sea to Shining Sea Memorial Trophy Dash, more commonly known as the Cannonball Run), my buddy Steve Gray and I got to know its primary organizers, Brock Yates Sr. and Brock Yates Jr. Of course, meeting celebrities at events intended to provide fans with opportunities to do so is anything but happenstance, but it is somehow comforting to discover that these larger-than-life figures are actually friendly people. That was certainly the case with both of the Yates men.

But what about those unplanned meetings with famous folks? I once saw Stephen King riding his motorcycle through an intersection in Millinocket, Maine. Although I have yet to actually meet him, I like knowing that he enjoys "regular guy" stuff. My wife, Kristy, and I met Henry Winkler at the old Borders Books location near Newark, Delaware many years ago. Granted, he was there for a book signing, but it was before his scheduled speaking time, and he was making small talk with the store manager while waiting. Kristy and I didn't know that a special event had been scheduled for that day. We had stopped in merely to purchase a gift card for my mother. Winkler was quite personable, and he chatted exclusively with the two of us for several minutes before jumping onto a table to stand and address those who had come to meet him and to buy his books.

My first random celebrity encounter occurred in the spring of 1985 when I was just nineteen years old. I had recently graduated automotive school, and I was working as a mechanic at Auto Doctor, a two-bay gas station and repair shop on Naaman's Road, north of Wilmington, Delaware. Weeks earlier, I had moved to a room in the basement of a friend's house in nearby Claymont. It was the second rented basement that I had called home.

The spring NASCAR race in Dover was a few days away, but my schedule didn't allow time to attend events such as this. I worked six days a week, and I did side work in the evenings and often on Sundays. My bushy red hair had grown much too large because I simply didn't have time to get it cut. Furthermore, my living expenses, tool payments, and student loan debt kept me broke. I couldn't afford to go to a stock car race. Even going out for a nice meal happened rarely. So, it was a special occurrence when on a beautiful spring day, my friend and coworker Jim and I went to nearby Stanley's Tavern for lunch. There we met up with our friend Billy, who owned the towing service that we used.

As we pulled into the parking lot at Stanley's, Jim and I spotted Bobby Allison's stock car parked near the door. It was the first stock car I had seen up close, and I was intrigued by its sanitary, yet bare-bones, all-business appearance. A guy wearing a Miller racing jacket, who introduced himself as Don, approached as Jim and I looked it over. When I asked if it was a real race car, Don pointed to a place near the driver's foot well where the tubing of the roll cage had been damaged in a crash the previous year. "Since it couldn't be raced again, we re-skinned it and now we use it as a show car," he explained. He was part of the Allison crew, and it was his job to haul the show car to pre-scheduled locations to display it prior to each race on the NASCAR circuit.

Bobby Allison, David Pearson, and Richard Petty were all childhood heroes of mine. Each year through the early and mid-1970s, I watched ABC's Wild World of Sports' coverage of the Daytona 500. Coincidentally, Brock Yates Sr. was a regular commentator. Prior to that day, I had never seen a NASCAR race in person. But there I stood, in the presence of a car that had been driven and crashed by one of my idols—a household name who was a mainstay of NASCAR royalty.

Don asked if we knew of a place nearby where he could have the trailer repaired. One of the leaf spring equalizer bolts on the large two-car enclosed hauler had been worn nearly in two, and he needed to have it replaced before it failed. Jim told him to bring it by our shop after work that night.

The Auto Doctor building sat on a triangular lot at the intersection of Naaman's and Darley Roads. This was prior to the widening of Naaman's Road, at which time the structure was leveled. The cramped lot was further encumbered by the gas pump island. When Don arrived that evening, he parked the trailer on one side of the island. He had to back the race car outside in order to lighten the trailer so that our jacks could lift it. Then he disconnected the trailer from the crew cab Chevy pick-up tow vehicle. While Jim and I worked on the trailer, Don drove to the Philadelphia Airport to pick up Davey Allison and his then-wife, Deborah. Meanwhile, the shop owner, Paul, talked with the throngs of folks who stopped by to take pictures of Bobby Allison's car.

In addition to working as a mechanic, Jim was a talented photographer. He called his wife, Cheryl, and asked her to bring his camera equipment as well as their kids, Jeremy and Stephanie, to the shop. Once we had finished our work on the trailer, Jim took several photos. Cheryl and the kids left before Don returned with the Allisons, and they took Jim's cameras and lenses home with them.

At that time, Davey was an up-and-coming driver—a star in the making. He had been racing successfully in the ARCA series for a few years, and that year he began driving in the Busch series. Despite his notoriety, he was friendly and humble. He struck me as a true southern gentleman who was genuinely grateful to Jim and me for our after-hours efforts. Tragically, eight years later, he succumbed to his injuries following a helicopter crash.

Don paid the bill and hooked up the trailer. He loaded the car, and then he and the Allisons headed for their motel. Jim and I closed up the shop, but as we were about to leave, the telephone rang. Don and the Allisons had made it to the bottom of the hill on Naaman's Road when the clutch in their truck failed. We called Billy, who hauled the Allison rig back to our shop.

The next morning, Jim brought his camera equipment back to work. Rather than have us repair the truck, the Allison team wisely opted to have it fixed by a company that offered a nationwide warranty. As I recall, Davey and Deborah rented a car and drove to Dover International Raceway. They paid Billy to use his rollback to take Don and the race car to each of its scheduled appearances that day. But first, Jim saw to it that we staged several photos with the Auto Doctor crew, Billy, Don, and the race car.

Although we didn't find out until after the race, the Allison crew had seen to it that there were race tickets on reserve for Jim and me at the gate. It is reassuring to find that our favorite celebrities are truly good people despite their fame, and that they appreciate the efforts of us everyday folks.

A Clone That Makes No Excuses

It was a sad day when seventeen-year-old Mark Shane missed an opportunity to buy a real '69 Camaro Z-28 for a price that was unbelievably attractive, even by 1986 standards. Further souring his experience, he explained that within a few weeks, "The kid who bought it wrapped it around a telephone pole." A short time afterward, however, Mark's luck changed. One afternoon he was on his way home from school when he spotted a red '69 Firebird convertible parked in front of a restaurant with a For Sale sign in the window. The asking price was 3,500 dollars, but he negotiated it down to 3,200 dollars. "It was a basic car with a 350 two-barrel engine and basic hubcaps." Although its red paint was somewhat faded and its top aged, it was in good condition overall. "I had some money saved up, and my parents helped me out by lending me the rest," he said. When he graduated high school a couple of months later, his grandmother paid off the remainder of what he owed. "That was her graduation present to me."

For the next five years, Mark drove the Firebird daily through all four seasons. "It wasn't very good in the snow, even with a few cinder blocks in the trunk for weight, but I drove it!" Along the way, he and his buddies repainted it and he replaced the top. "It looked pretty good considering we repainted it in a barn. It was a good twenty-footer," Mark said. In order to preserve his car, he retired it from daily use in 1991, relegating it to fun weekend cruiser status instead. "My cousin really loves this car, and he asked if I would drive him and his wife around on their wedding day. Through the years, there have been lots of family connections with it.

"I moved into my house in 2000. The car had some rot under the windshield, and I thought since that panel was only spot-welded in, it would be an easy fix. But I had to remove the windshield, and then the dashboard. It seemed that everything I had to get to meant removing a whole lot of other stuff. And then I thought, I might as well replace the heater core since I can get to it now, and the blower motor too. Finally, I decided to blow the whole car apart." An eight-and-a-half-year project ensued. "I had parts stashed all over the house, but I had things grouped together. All of the interior stuff was in one area, for example. Parts were everywhere, but I could find anything I needed."

One day, a friend of Mark's called and offered him a different engine. "My buddy said, 'Do you want a 455?' I said, 'Yeah, how much?' He said, 'Do you want a 455?' Again, I said, 'Yeah, how much?' He asked, 'DO YOU WANT A 455?' I said, 'YES!'" And so it was that Mark scored a free 455 to replace his original 350. Around that time, his plans changed from simply refurbishing his old ride, and he decided to replicate one of the eight Trans-Am convertibles that had been built by the factory in 1969.

Mark met his wife, Pam, in 2003, and they were married in 2006. Because his convertible was still in pieces, they could not use it in their wedding. "Pam is a car girl. She helped put it together, and she also told me to make a list of all of the things we still needed. We took it to a body shop on her birthday, and we picked it up on our first anniversary. She is the one who gave me the push to finally get it finished."

Mark and Pam completed the Firebird's transformation in April 2009. Its first major car show was in Carlisle, Pennsylvania shortly afterward. "There were still a few little things left to do, and I didn't have it fully detailed, but when I rolled across the show field, people just stared. After I parked, they all walked toward me like zombies muttering, 'Oh my God! A real Trans-Am convertible!' I said, 'No, no, it's just a clone,'" Mark laughed. "I would never try to misrepresent this car as a real Trans Am convertible. That would be automotive blasphemy."

Although it looked great, the 455 proved problematic. "I could never get it to run right, and I could never time it properly," he said. In addition, with the stock Turbo Hydramatic 350 transmission and the 3.73 to one rear axle ratio, highway cruising was not much fun because the engine strained at high speeds. "We went to a show in Frederick, Maryland, and rather than drive it, I towed it with a tow dolly. Towing it that far with the rear wheels on the ground destroyed the transmission."

Eventually, Mark and Pam sought the help of Rob's Rod Shop in Downingtown, Pennsylvania to get the mechanicals sorted out. According to owner Rob McCall, "Mark used all good parts when he built the 455, but they weren't well matched. With the cylinder heads he had, the compression ratio worked out to be thirteen and a half to one." Working with Pontiac expert Paul Spotts of Spotts Performance, Rob's chief mechanic Jon Kersey reassembled the engine with a combination of parts that netted 472 cubic inches of displacement and a pump gas friendly compression ratio of 9.3 to one. While this was going on, Sean Wiley at Dynamic Transmissions built a later 200 4-R transmission which includes an overdrive ratio for easy highway cruising. Once the engine and transmission were installed, Jon and Rob added a Holley Sniper electronic fuel injection system.

"My wife could never start the car when it had a carburetor. She used to say, 'It hates me!' But she has no problem now that it has fuel injection. Anybody could start it now," Mark said. Since its transformation, Pam also enjoys spending time in the driver's seat. "She drives it to shows, and she's not afraid to chirp the tires," Mark laughed.

One hiccup arose when Rob attempted to run the Firebird on his dynamometer. The transmission had been built to withstand 500 horsepower in street trim, but street tires seldom grip the pavement well at that power level. The resulting tire slippage helps to mitigate drivetrain breakage. On the hub-mounted dyno, however, there is no tire slippage, so all drivetrain components are subjected to the maximum torque produced by the engine. As the speed and load increased, the torque proved too great for the transmission's input shaft. "There was a loud bang, and then the transmission started hemorrhaging fluid!" Mark said. "It was a one-hundred percent clean break." Sean replaced the failed input shaft with an upgraded part, and the drivetrain has held up well since then.

Mark and Pam live in southeastern Pennsylvania. He explained, "We built this car to drive, and with the overdrive transmission, highway cruising is a dream! We have driven it to the Ocean City, Maryland cruise several times, shows in Carlisle, Pennsylvania, and we have even driven it to Rhode Island." Aside from the tow dolly incident, it has never been trailered. "If this was a real million-and-a-half dollar Trans Am convertible, I wouldn't be driving it. That's assuming I could even afford own it."

About the long build, Mark said, "I learned a lot by doing things—what to do, and what not to do." Since its completion in 2009, he and Pam have been making memories not just for themselves, but for others as well. "We went to Outback Steak House for dinner one night, and we parked by the door. The hostesses spotted the car, and they asked if they could take a picture. I said, 'Sure! Do you want to sit in it?' They couldn't believe I would let them do that. I said, 'It's okay. I'm not going to give you the keys!' We do the same thing at car shows. If a kid really likes it, we let him sit in it. That's what it's all about.

"We go to all kinds of local shows, and we have won several trophies, but we go to hang out with our buddies," Mark said. Typically, awards are given out at the end of a show. "It's nice to get your name called, but it's not about getting a trophy. Besides, you can't win every time. We hang out and have a good time. We meet nice people. That's what I like about it. The car makes us introduce ourselves. We also re-meet people who we haven't seen in years. It's fun."

In addition, Mark said, "It's obviously more than a car. It's a part of me. It's a link to my young adulthood days as well as to my family. My wife always tells me, 'You get a grin on your face whenever you are driving this car.' It's my happy place.

A Man and His Superbird

It was an ordinary day at work late in 1991. I was a 26-year-old flat-rate mechanic working in a Dodge dealership, but I was firmly rooted in the automotive hobby as well. At home I had just put the finishing touches on the 3 ½ car garage that I'd built over the previous eight months to house my '68 Dart GT, '68 Dart GTS convertible, and '67 Belvedere.

As lunchtime approached, the Snap-On man arrived and handed me several outdated calendars. He said, "I found these while I was cleaning out the garage over the weekend. They aren't much good as calendars anymore, but they have some really cool car pictures that I thought you'd appreciate." I thanked him and laid them on the side cabinet of my toolbox. The January photograph of the top calendar happened to be of a white Plymouth Superbird.

Sometime later that morning Larry, the mechanic who worked in the next bay, wandered over and spotted the Superbird. Larry was my age, but he had been born and raised in the Bahamas. Although he was aware of American muscle cars, he hadn't grown up in the car culture the way many of us did. He and I were good friends, although we talked a lot of smack and routinely played jokes on each other. He said, "Look at that big ugly car! That thing is so big you could live in it!" He continued his rant peppered with insults and expletives, eventually mentioning, "I know where there's one like that." I was certain he was either mistaken or he was spinning this yarn for his own amusement, but he insisted. I asked if the car he was talking about had the tall rear wing and the pointed nose. He said it did. I called his bluff. He said, "I'm serious!"

I still had doubts, but Larry insisted. He agreed to take me to the car. Unfortunately, we both worked second jobs and we couldn't coordinate our schedules. After two weeks of trying, I asked him to give me directions.

The following Saturday afternoon I drove to a decaying neighborhood near Wilmington, Delaware. I thought, No way is there a Superbird here. Larry got me good this time! Just then I rounded a bend in the narrow street, and parked at the curb half a block away was a derelict white Superbird! Its damaged nose had been troweled full of body filler, its headlights were stuck open, its vinyl top had been slashed, and it had other minor damage, but it was the car Larry had promised I'd find. I parked my truck across the street and circled the 'Bird, peering underneath. The oil pan was badly dented, but the Dana 60 rear axle was in place, the black bucket seat interior was reasonably intact, and the factory Pistol Grip shifter stretched upward from the floor. The Superbird-specific windshield and rear window moldings were also in place. A current registration sticker was affixed to the corner of the vanity tag that read BUCK.

I could barely contain my excitement as I scurried up the walkway and knocked on the door of the single-story flat amid a row of identical connected houses. After a few minutes of knocking, the man in the adjacent home opened his door. He eyed me for a moment, apparently concluding that I did not belong in that neighborhood. "You're here about the car, aren't you?" I nodded. He said, "Don't waste your time. Lots of people have tried to buy that car, but the old guy will never sell it. He's home, but he's almost deaf. He can't hear you knocking."

I thanked him and headed for my truck intending to write a note and leave it on the windshield. For some reason I peered under the front of the car again, only to hear angry shouts from behind me. I stood and turned to see an elderly gentleman moving toward me slowly and stiffly, presumably due to advanced arthritis. He wore a shirt and pants that had gone out of style decades earlier, and his gray hair had been stained yellow by Bryl Crème.

I quickly apologized. I explained that I had knocked on his door, but he hadn't answered, and that I was only looking at his car. He calmed down quickly and said he thought I might be stealing parts from it. I assured him that was not the case. I expressed my love of Superbirds. I also mentioned the cars I owned, and that led him to tell me about his car.

As I recall, his name was George. He and his wife had bought their home many decades earlier when this now-rotting neighborhood had been a quaint little community full of friendly neighbors, most of whom were raising children. George worked for the DuPont Corporation as either an engineer or a chemist. He had been a NASCAR fan from its earliest days when it was known as Grand National racing, and he had followed the technical advances spawned by the competition between manufacturers as the years progressed. He was especially interested in the aerodynamic developments of the late 1960s, which ultimately led to the creation of the Dodge Charger Daytona in 1969 and the Plymouth Road Runner Superbird the following year.

In order to homologate the Superbird for racing in NASCAR, Chrysler Corporation was required to build two Superbirds for every dealer, which equated to 1920 cars. It is common knowledge that, although they were very competitive on the racetrack, Superbirds were not well-received by the public due to their outlandish styling and high cost. Many languished on dealer lots for years. George, however, was determined to own a Superbird even before they were released to the public. "I knew what it was. I had researched them, and I wanted one."

Although they both loved children, George and his wife never had any of their own. Instead, they befriended the kids in their neighborhood. Of course, the Superbird was a hit with them. "Sometimes on a Saturday afternoon we would load up as many kids as we could fit in the car and take them out for ice cream. The kids loved riding up and down New

Castle Avenue, and they really liked it whenever somebody wanted to pick a race with me."

As we talked, he explained that the word BUCK on his license plate was actually his nickname, which had been derived from his last name.

I don't remember how, but our conversation eventually strayed from the car to times earlier in George's life, including his service during World War II. He related several noteworthy as well as some funny incidents from those days. As he talked, it seemed that he gradually stood a little bit straighter and his voice took on a more robust, less gravelly tone. Despite the arthritis, his hand gestures also became more fluid as the years melted away.

When talk of the car resumed, George said that his wife had become ill in the 'seventies, and that he had retired so that he could care for her. His nephew had been using the Superbird during that time, and one morning while rounding an off-ramp on I-295 in New Jersey, he hit a patch of ice and punched the nose into a guardrail. He spoke in a matter-of-fact tone. Even if he had been angry with his nephew at the time, he was over it now.

As George spoke I couldn't help thinking, In the context of today's world, he has no idea what he's got! I suspected that he thought the Superbird was now a nearly forgotten anecdote in the annals of automotive history. On the contrary, by the early 'nineties it had become a highly collectible car, and one that I would have loved to have had in my own garage. The first wave of the muscle car craze had washed over the hobby in the late 'eighties. At that time, a year after the Gulf War had begun, muscle car prices were up significantly from where they had been five years earlier, and high-profile cars like Superbirds were riding the crest of that wave. I was shocked that this car was sitting outdoors on a crowded urban street and that George trusted all who drove past to remain attentive enough not to accidentally sideswipe it.

I realized that to George, his Superbird represented over twenty years of his life and the final years that he had spent with his wife. It was a reminder of the last of the happy times they had shared—a token that he would cling to indefinitely. I doubted if any of the kids, now grown, who had gone for ice cream in the big white 'Bird still stopped around to see him, but I don't think it mattered. The car spurred his memories of those times, and that was enough. I believed that he was oblivious to the collector car community's newfound infatuation with Chrysler Corporation's winged cars. Furthermore, I believed it wouldn't have mattered to him if he had known the public's opinion had done an about-face and that the once-shunned Superbird was now a highly sought collector car.

Then George uttered a sentence that destroyed my foregone conclusions. "I have everything to restore this car." Sensing my disbelief he said, "I have a new nose. I have quarter panels. I even have all of the upholstery and a new vinyl top." My mouth fell agape. "That stuff is from Legendary. I assume you've heard of them?" Indeed, I had. Legendary Auto Interiors was a relatively new company that offered high quality reproduction soft trim, and already I had spent hundreds of dollars with them. George continued, "I joined the Winged Warriors car club several years ago, and they helped me find a lot of what I need." I knew that the Winged Warriors club was comprised of Dodge Daytona and Plymouth Superbird owners.

Before I could ask, he volunteered, "The only reason I haven't restored it is because I don't know who I can trust to do the work." He also explained that he preferred to park it in front of his home where he could keep an eye on it rather than store it in a rented garage where it would lie at the mercy of thieves and vandals. "I wouldn't know if anything happened to it until it was too late." Looking at it from his perspective, and thinking of how he had taken alarm when I had peered under it, I understood.

I asked him if he would ever consider selling it, to which he replied, "No. I'd like to restore it and give it to my nephew. But I'll never sell it."

For the next year or two I drove by from time to time, and eventually George moved the Superbird inside the fence that surrounded his yard. His second car, a Corvair, continued to sit on the street. Then one day I saw that both cars were gone, and the meager contents of George's home had been moved to the front yard. I concluded that he had passed away.

Five years later, I heard a rumor from an unreliable source that George's nephew had inherited his Superbird and all of its parts. Seeing only dollar signs, he had sold off everything as fast as he could to numerous buyers. More recently I heard from another source that the car and all of its parts had been tucked away, and that its restoration might soon get underway. In either case, I'm sure it will be restored eventually if it hasn't been already. I only hope that its history isn't lost in the process, and that George's memory is preserved and remains linked to his 'Bird. The history of the car and the story of George's life are truly one and the same.

Author's Note: After this story appeared in Cruising Magazine, George's nephew contacted me. He had inherited George's Superbird and all of the parts that George had accumulated for it, and he had, in fact, stored everything away. Few people knew what had become of George's car, and even fewer had seen it since his death. Restorations are expensive, and George's nephew was not yet in a position to restore the car properly, but he hoped to do so one day soon.

A Woods-Dwelling '53 Chevy

It was the summer of 1977. America's Bicentennial had passed, Jimmy Carter was in the White House, and Heart's <u>Barracuda</u> seemed to play endlessly on the radio. My buddy Kevin Pampuch and I were twelve years old, and we spent much of the summer riding our stripped-down bicycles on the trails through the fields and woods near our neighborhood, which sat mid-way between Newark and Wilmington, Delaware just off Kirkwood Highway. It would be another year before we would graduate to dirt bikes and go-karts.

One day, while exploring the trails behind St. Mark's church and high school, we discovered an old Chevy that had been abandoned in the woods years earlier. The body was peppered with bullet holes and the windows had been blown out. Somebody had removed the engine and transmission, presumably before dumping the carcass in the woods. The caved-in roof had a gaping rust hole; time and the elements had ravaged the seats, reducing them to bare, rusty springs. I studied the grille, and when I got home, I consulted the Chilton repair manual that my father had purchased to help him service our '63 Corvair. The Chilton manual covered domestic models from 1953-1963, and I determined that "our" Chevy was a 1953 model.

The fact that we had little automotive knowledge and even less money did nothing to dampen our enthusiasm. We had each built dozens of plastic model kits, and we were adept at modifying these cars to suit our own tastes. Leftover parts from various kits found their way onto other cars; stock pre-war Ford bodies became dirt track racers while '50s classics became "gasser" style drag race cars with blowers and multiple carburetors protruding from crudely hacked holes in their hoods. Many of these cars sat on shelves in our bedrooms. Some succumbed to the damage sustained in the demolition derbies that we sometimes held, while others met with destruction at the ends of long strings which we tied to our bicycles.

Of course, we had to buy these models as well as the paint and glue needed to assemble them. We each had sufficient mechanical aptitude to keep our lawnmowers running so we could earn the money we needed to buy these model kits and the related supplies. We also honed our mechanical skills and spent a fair portion of our grass cutting money keeping our bicycles going despite the abuse we lavished upon them. We weren't naïve to the fact that we had a lot to learn about cars, but we remained steadfast in our belief that, between the two of us, we had a sufficient knowledge base to take on a project like the Chevy. It was our plan that by the time we obtained our driver's licenses, we would have an operable car to share.

Today, Kevin and I would each consider this car too far gone to revive. Truth be told, it wouldn't have even been a good parts car, for I don't recall any of its pieces being in a condition suitable to repair a road-going example. Furthermore, we had no idea who the legal owner was or how to obtain the necessary paperwork to own and register it. But none of that mattered. We would tackle what we could now, and we would figure out the rest as we went along. Our determination and hard work, combined with a few lucky breaks that were sure to come our way, would enable us to see this project through.

Parts procurement was one of our first considerations. We knew where an engine had been discarded in a creek nearby. We didn't know what kind of engine it was or what was wrong with it, nor did we know how we would retrieve it, but we figured that simply locating it was a starting point. We also found what we thought would be a suitable transmission in a similar condition, though I'm not sure if it occurred to us that it probably wouldn't bolt up to the engine. Our first objective, however, was to replace the roof. We reasoned that until we made the car weather-tight, the mechanicals were moot.

Fortunately, nearby sat the roof and a few other body panels from a Mercury Montclair. I recognized these sheet metal bits as such, for there was another Montclair parked in the apartment complex near Kevin's house. We measured the Montclair roof and deemed it close enough in size to fit the Chevy. I didn't know how we would come up with a windshield or any of the other windows that would fit both the Chevy body and the Montclair roof, but Kevin said he thought we could make windows out of Plexiglas. To me, his idea sounded like a sure-fire solution.

On a hot and humid morning, Kevin and I each borrowed our fathers' hacksaws without their knowledge, and we met at the Chevy. With dogged determination, we hacked through the A-pillars, B-pillars, and C-pillars. This task was complicated by the tree that had grown against the left side of the car at the rear-most roof pillar. Even so, later that afternoon, we stood on the dashboard, grasped the roof, and flipped it over the back of the car. We watched as it fell into the ravine aft of the rear bumper.

I do not remember test-fitting the Montclair roof on the Chevy. It is possible that we did, but more than four decades later I would say it is likely that our barely pubescent bodies lacked the strength necessary to lift the roof and position it atop the Chevy body. I also don't remember how we had planned to attach the roof to the body. What I do remember is that we had a difference of opinion. I was intent on realizing our initial plan. Kevin, however, was more grounded than I was. He had begun to accept the reality of our plight, and he realized that we would probably never get the car roadworthy. Recently, he reminded me that we thought the rear of the car had sunken into the ground. Upon closer inspection, we discovered that the rear axle was missing. How would we put wheels on it? How would we move it from the edge of the ravine if we couldn't make it roll?

We certainly couldn't raise the rear of the car with a bumper jack. At once, our progress ground to a halt.

Kevin and I each acquired our first cars when we were fifteen. Mine was the '64 Dodge Dart that had belonged to my great-aunt Betty, while his was the '69 Camaro that his grandparents had bought new. I removed the ailing push-button automatic transmission from my car, and I replaced it with a floor-shifted three-speed manual transmission from a Plymouth Duster prior to my sixteenth birthday. A few months later, Kevin and I removed the Powerglide automatic transmission from his Camaro and replaced it with a Muncie M-21 four-speed.

After high school, Kevin went to college in Virginia while I commuted to an automotive school in Pennsylvania. Our careers took us in different directions, though our personal lives have had many parallels. They included marriage, divorce, family, college, homeownership, and a plethora of other milestones at differing points on our individual highways of life. Although we saw each other infrequently, through the years he and I have both owned and/or built numerous vehicles. Our skillsets overlap, but there are major differences. Kevin is a fantastic welder, fabricator, and machinist. I enjoy building engines, transmissions, suspensions, and electrical systems. One of Kevin's current "toys" is an old-school hot-rod that he built from a carefully selected assortment of early 1930s Ford parts. I have always been drawn to the '60s and '70s Chrysler vehicles. I usually modify them to maintain nearly stock appearances while improving their performance, road manners, and reliability. But what Kevin and I have in common is that we have spent our lives immersed in the automotive culture. We are no less enthusiastic about cars now than we were on the day we discovered that old Chevy. Our lust for automobiles has infiltrated most other areas of our lives too. Our homes include garage and shop space, we attend various cruises, swap meets, and racing events regularly, and most of our friendships have come about through our automotive connections. Of course, we are still friends today.

As a teen, I lamented that we gave up on that old Chevy. But even though it didn't transport us through our high school years, I know now that it served a far greater purpose. It launched two twelve-year-old kids into lifetime obsessions with automobiles, and it gave us each a glimpse of what awaited us in the decades ahead.

A Young Woman and Her Oldsmobile

Adrianna Straub didn't set out to become well known in automotive circles. But even if many folks don't recognize her name, those who have followed the coverage of the Muscle Cars and Corvette Nationals in recent years have seen her, and fans of the Pure Stock Drags racing series certainly know who she is. She has also captured attention at some of the other major automotive events in the northeast and Midwest, including those in Carlisle, Pennsylvania.

Adrianna is part of a tight-knit family in Michigan. She said, "I grew up with classic cars. My grandpa, my dad, and my uncle were all into classic cars and drag racing. My grandpa drag raced a '69 Dart GTS, and my dad and uncle helped work on it. When I was small, Grandpa would buckle me up in my booster seat and I would cruise with him to diners and the ice cream shop. I cruised with my dad and uncle too. When they did burn-outs, I would laugh. My siblings got into it as well. My mom and dad often went to swap meets, and we kids participated from the time we were six or seven years old. We went to shows all over Michigan, including those on the Upper Peninsula and the Frankenmuth Autofest. Also, I often went with Dad to look at cars and parts."

Eventually, Adrianna's grandfather retired from racing, and he sold his Dart to a friend. Adrianna's father, Richard Straub, and her uncle, Carl Straub, got into the racing action in their own cars. In addition, while she was in high school, Adrianna was often seen driving an orange '70

Olds 442. "I drove it to the dances and to prom," she said. "I really connected with that car."

Unfortunately, Adrianna's grandfather passed away days before she graduated high school. "That was quite difficult. Dad suggested that I try drag racing to help me cope with the loss, but I didn't feel comfortable. There were no girls racing at our track." That changed two years later. "I came across another girl, Victoria, and her sister, who both drag raced. Then I felt comfortable trying it myself. I was twenty when I started drag racing, and I knew right away that I was made to do it. It was relaxing. Knowing that it was a family thing, it came naturally. My family had faith in me when I didn't have faith in myself."

Her first race was at the Pure Stock Drags, held annually in September at the Mid-Michigan Motorplex. This event is open to muscle cars that are nearly all stock, right down to the tires, which must be the same style and size as those installed by the factory. "I started racing the Oldsmobile. It's an automatic, and I already had a feel for the car," she said. "I only had two weeks to practice—learning the tree, using both feet to stage, and learning the method of doing the burn-out. I did quite well in the Olds. My dad and uncle were surprised! People were amazed at how well I did, and they referred to the Olds and me as 'The Match.'"

Adrianna raced successfully for a couple of years before her grandfather's friend, who had purchased the Dart, passed away. "The family wanted to sell the car, and they offered it to us first. My parents had to raise the money quickly, so they sold the Olds to a close friend in New York." While it broke her heart to lose her car against her will, she said, "When money is tight, you do what you have to do. You make sacrifices for what is important to the family." Even so, those sacrifices are seldom easy. "We sold the Olds to get the Dart back, but that put a damper on things."

As her father, Richard, explained, "There's a lot of difference between the Olds and the Dart. The Dart has a leaf spring and torsion bar suspension (unlike the Oldsmobile's coil spring suspension), and it takes a lot of finesse to get a good launch." The engines are quite different too. The Olds is equipped with a 455, which made ample low-end torque, while the Dart has a high-revving 340.

Adrianna said, "I love the Dart because of my history growing up with the car. I still love it, but I really connected with the Oldsmobile." Although she was initially devastated over the loss of the Olds, she and her family tried to remain positive. "My dad said, 'Your grandpa would love to see you driving that car.' It hadn't been on the track in twenty years, but my grandma got to see me race it. It also makes my parents happy to see," Adrianna said. But all was not good initially, for issues arose one after another. "Problems would pop up and I wouldn't get a good run. The first year I raced it at the Pure Stock Drags, we went through six belts in one day. Then we had cooling system problems. I thought, maybe it's a sign that Grandpa doesn't want me racing his car. I didn't get a good run until this year, and then it ran really well. We finally got it fixed toward the end of racing season." Still, the Dart could not fill the void in Adrianna's heart left by the Oldsmobile.

Due to her success racing the Olds in the Pure Stock Drags, the Oldsmobile Club of Ontario asked her to be their Brand Ambassador. "I had to explain to them that the Olds had been sold, but that I was looking for another one. Still, they said they wanted me to be their Brand Ambassador, so I agreed."

As a regular Pure Stock Drags competitor, she met photographer Tim Costello, and the two quickly became friends. Tim introduced her to Bob Ashton, Managing Member of the Muscle Car and Corvette Nationals, a prestigious car show that occurs every November in Chicago. "Bob asked if we could come to MCACN. He also asked me about modeling in '60s and '70s clothes. He thought it would be a fun thing to do at the event, and my parents and I thought it would be really cool. It was a big hit! People really like it, and they are amazed that I have a car there. My family and I help Tim and Bob by going in early and doing whatever they need. We have also helped Tim with parts for his car. We treat each other like family. We check up on each other often, and we have grown really close."

Being a premier show, many restorers and owners choose MCACN as the place to unveil their recently completed restorations. During the 2021 show, Adrianna was asked to help unveil one car in particular. As she began to remove the cover, she observed that it was an orange Oldsmobile 442. "It was a lot like my old car, but this one looked new!" But as the cover was rolled up the hood and windshield and then across the roof, an object on the seat caught her eye. "My helmet was sitting on the seat. That's when it really hit me! The announcer asked me, 'Do you recognize this car?' That's when I lost it. I couldn't talk. My parents were crying too. Later, Dad told me he worked things out so that he was able to buy it back. My parents had it freshened up with new paint, new tires, and lots of other issues fixed. I knew nothing about it!"

Adrianna is grateful to her family and everyone else who had a hand in pulling off this surprise. The 2022 racing season will be busy for the Straub family. Adrianna explained, "My mom got involved with racing after seeing me do it. Dad started pushing my sixteen-year-old sister to get involved, and now she loves it. My uncle used to race, but now he coaches me, helps with the cars, and takes photos. He likes to watch from the sidelines." Going forward, Richard Straub will be racing the Dart, Adrianna's mother Carolyn will be racing a Super Bee, her sister Caroline will be racing a Demon, and Adrianna will be back behind the wheel of her Oldsmobile. For the Straubs, racing is truly a family affair.

Bozzie's Bee

There are many reasons we develop a fondness for certain cars. It might be the rarity of a particular car that attracts us, its aggressive styling, striking color combination, or perhaps its performance options. Often a certain car takes us back in time and allows us to relive the past, and sometimes that car was owned by a family member and has, through the years, become a family member itself. Mike Boswell's red 1971 Hemi Super Bee meets all of these criteria.

The story begins on a hot summer day in 1971. Mike's older brother, Rich, went to Kirkwood Dodge in Wilmington, Delaware to purchase a 1969 Charger Daytona that was being traded in on a Dodge "Dude" pick-up. At the last minute the owner of the Daytona came to his senses and backed out of the deal. Disappointed but not too discouraged, the elder Boswell instead ordered a brand-new Hemi Charger. Despite how it might have seemed at the time, luck was on his side, for he placed his order during the last week that the Hemi option was offered in the Charger. In addition to the Hemi, Rich's list of options included the Super Trac Pack and not much else. The Ramcharger fresh air hood, power steering, and power disc brakes were included with the Hemi engine, but Rich specified no radio, air conditioning, console, or even bucket seats. Instead, he opted for the standard bench seat and column-mounted shifter to save weight.

The Boswell family lived in Newark, Delaware not far from Chrysler's Newark assembly plant and shipping depot. As the weeks rolled by, eleven-year-old Mike rode his bicycle to the plant daily to see if the car had arrived in the transfer yard. When it finally did come in, it was adorned with Super Bee emblems and graphics. Until then the Boswells had no idea there was such a thing as a Charger Super Bee. "Prior to 1971, the Charger and Super Bee were separate models, but in 1971 they combined them," Mike explained.

Having been relegated to a wheelchair following a car accident some time earlier, Rich had the Charger fitted with hand controls after it arrived at the dealership. Then, upon taking delivery, he went racing! At first the Charger Super Bee competed in "D Strictly Stock," a showroom stock class that permitted no modifications at all. In his first season Rich won eight races, including the Maryland State Championship—all with hand controls!

Of course, the big red 'Bee saw some street action in its early years too, and a pre-teen Mike always got to ride along. "Rich had to take me along. If we stopped somewhere, he needed me to get his wheelchair out of the trunk," he explains. He also spent many hours helping Rich work on the car. "One time I was helping him replace the header gaskets. I was holding the gasket in place while he installed the header from underneath. He pinched my finger between the header and the head, and he wouldn't drop the header down so I could get my finger out!"

Throughout the 1970s the Super Bee saw limited use, and it received a few modifications including a cool can, headers, a line lock, and slicks. Over the 'Bee's lifetime the Dana 60 has housed four different ratios, the transmission has housed a forward pattern manual valve body and a 4400 RPM stall speed torque converter, and for a while the rear was suspended by Super Stock drag race-oriented leaf springs.

Due to his injuries, winters were especially difficult for Rich. In 1981 he moved to Florida and Mike acquired the 'Bee. At that time the odometer showed just 4,000 miles. In its modified state it posted its best run of 11.55 seconds at 116 MPH, after which Mike was quickly escorted to the gate for lack of a roll bar. In pure stock trim its best run was 12.39 at 107 MPH. According to Mike, "It made a 12.56 pass in about 1982 or '83 with six people in the car. That's one of its most amazing feats ever. It had to weigh 6,000 pounds!" That's not much of an exaggeration considering its 4100-pound curb weight.

In 1984 he returned the car to its stock state, and a few years later Cars and Parts magazine published a five-page spread on the 'Bee, but its racing days weren't over yet. From 1994 through 1997 Mike competed in several National Muscle Car Association events before finally retiring the 'Bee from racing for good.

In 1971 only 22 Hemi Super Bees were built—thirteen with automatic transmissions and nine with four-speeds. Mike's is one of the thirteen auto transmission-equipped cars, and possibly the last Hemi Super Bee ever built. Of course, this isn't news to Mike. He has known the production figures for most of the time he has owned the car, but this one was bought to be raced, so despite its rarity that's exactly what he did.

Even so, with the second muscle car craze in full swing during the late '90s, he realized that it was foolish to risk a failed connecting rod punching a window in the side of the original numbers-matching block. There comes a time when the value and historical significance of such a car can no longer be ignored despite its intended purpose.

One weekend night many years ago, Mike took me for a ride in the 'Bee. We drove to the back of a deserted industrial park not far from his home. There, he turned the car around, stopped, applied the line lock, and heated the rear tires. After spinning them sufficiently to make them sticky, he rolled forward, applied the brake, and brought the engine speed up, thus loading the torque converter. When he released the brake, he simultaneously floored the accelerator. The car rocketed forward as my head snapped back. Seconds later, the shift light on the tachometer flashed brightly, and Mike clicked the column-mounted shifter into second gear. When the light illuminated again, he clicked the shifter into third gear. Moments later, he backed off the accelerator and brought the car down to a reasonable speed. All the while, he sat as calmly as if he had been surfing channels while seated on his couch.

Two things surprised me about the car's Jekyll and Hyde personality. First, the Super Bee drove like the low mileage car that it was. There were no vibrations, squeaks, nor rattles. It accelerated and braked smoothly, its demeanor belying the monster that lived within. When Mike chose to unleash that monster, it proved powerful, but refined. There was no squirrelly movement nor unruly behavior. And when he had lifted his foot, Mr. Hyde instantly transformed back into Dr. Jekyll.

Today the 'Bee is a regular sight at area cruises and car shows, and it has been featured in at least two other magazines. Having logged just 19,000 miles it still wears its original paint. Mike still has all of the paperwork including the window sticker and the cancelled check signed by Rich more than fifty years ago.

Fathers, Sons, and Super Cars

Most of the people who knew my father would not have mistaken him for an automotive enthusiast. He lived his life as a devoted family man who supported us by working for a large cooperation in Wilmington, Delaware. When he was downsized more than thirty years ago he fell back on his second career as a Certified Public Accountant. Unbeknownst to many of his co-workers he had earned CPA status some fifteen years earlier and had been doing accounting and tax work part-time ever since. Through it all he attended church on Sundays and family events regularly, and he donated countless hours to my Boy Scout troop, both as an adult leader and as Scoutmaster. He remained active with the troop even after I had attained the rank of Eagle Scout and moved on to the next phase of my life. His involvement with automobiles consisted only of the maintenance and light repairs required to keep the family iron mobile, provided they could be performed in the driveway on a Saturday morning. Working on cars was a chore, not something he did for joy. A frugal man, he was more concerned with gas mileage than with horsepower.

Or was he? As a child I always looked forward to the days when our cars needed the oil changed. During those times he would relate stories to me of his one automotive indulgence, a 1957 Plymouth Fury with the Golden Commando engine topped by two Carter WCFB four-barrel carburetors, or simply "dual quads" as he put it. During the time that he and my mother dated, he had owned the Fury for a mere six months before transmission trouble sidelined it in favor of a Corvair. Even so, the numerous adventures and misadventures he had experienced with that car during its short tenure could almost fill a lifetime.

Yes, my father was a closet car enthusiast. Throughout the latter part of his life, I was baffled by his staunch unwillingness to cater to his automotive desires or to own another Plymouth similar to his Fury. By contrast, I still own the car I built and drove as a young adult, and my wife and I own several others that we lusted for as youths. For most of my life, and for reasons unknown to me, my father disapproved of my automotive conquests, though he finally reached the point of acceptance. At last, he realized it is an integral part of who I am rather than something that would derail me, preventing me from becoming the man I might otherwise be. Though I share most of his beliefs and values, this is one area where we remained at opposite extremes. Still, secretly he always loved riding in my cars, and I have always known that his memory of his old Fury was the benchmark by which he judged the performance of all other cars.

My father was the most honest person I have ever known, and I never doubted the stories he told of his Fury. Although he would never intentionally embellish his recounting of various street races, I also know that time has a way of distorting our personal flight recorders. It is human nature to remember things as better than they really were, and memory can be altered by emotion, especially over a span of many years. No doubt the Fury was a terror in its day, but that was more than a decade before the pinnacle of the muscle car wars. Surely the Fury could not measure up to Detroit's hottest offerings during the late 'sixties. I have never found any drag test data from the various magazine reviews, but I knew the engine was rated at 290 horsepower. Dividing that into the 3595-pound shipping weight yields 12.40 pounds per horsepower.

In 1990 I purchased a '68 Dodge Dart GTS powered by a 340. It was my first true muscle car. At 275 horsepower and 3038 pounds shipping weight its power to weight ratio computed to 11.05 pounds per horsepower. While my father was impressed by how it ran, I knew by his face that he didn't think it could hang with his Fury.

As the years went on I built several other cars including a '64 Dart with a healthy 360, a '68 Dart with a 383, a '68 Plymouth Belvedere police car with a 400, and a '70 Dart with a supercharged 360. The supercharged Dart was understandably in a class by itself, but none of the naturally aspirated cars could measure up to my father's memory of his Fury. I found this amusing, and for me it became a game of sorts. I wasn't obsessed with trying to outdo my old man, but I was certain that the cars I was building were all much faster than his Fury had actually been. Yet I also knew there was no way to compete with a man's memory of the car he had cherished in his youth some fifty years earlier.

Only my wife's '68 Road Runner (335 horsepower, 3405-pound shipping weight, 10.16 pounds per horsepower) came close. Car and Driver magazine had tested a similar Road Runner in the standing quarter mile, posting 15.0 seconds at 96 MPH, and I achieved 14.6 seconds at 94 MPH at Cecil County Dragway in her car. One sunny weekend afternoon after a hard run approaching triple digits my father remarked, "I think this thing might just about keep up with my Fury."

One sunny Saturday afternoon I visited my parents after leaving a car show not far from their home in Wilmington, Delaware. It was the first time they would see my '67 GTX and I was eager to take my father for a ride. Car and Driver magazine had tested a similar car, posting 14.4 seconds at 98 MPH in the quarter mile. I had piloted mine to a best of 14.1 seconds at 96 MPH. At 375 horsepower and 3535 pounds shipping weight the GTX boasts only 9.43 pounds per horsepower, but its 440 cubic inches belt out 480 foot-pounds of torque. While it is undeniably faster than a '57 Fury, I was fairly certain it was not faster than my father's recollection of his '57 Fury, and that was fine with me.

We pulled out of the neighborhood and onto a secondary road. I straightened the wheel, then stomped the accelerator from a roll. The Torque flite automatic transmission jumped back to first gear and the skinny fourteen-inch tires howled in protest as the tail of the GTX wagged to the right and then the left. "Damn!" was my father's only comment. After turning left onto the main road, I pummeled the accelerator again, but this time from a higher speed so as not to annihilate the tires. The big green Plymouth squatted slightly on its haunches, lifted its nose with pride and shot forward, pressing us into our seats. It moaned loudly through the air cleaner as it sucked in a rush of atmosphere while bellowing from its exhaust. After releasing the accelerator, I glanced at my father and found him grinning. "This damned thing would run circles around my Fury!"

I have never felt the need to outdo my father, nor was it my intention to crush his memory of his own super car. Even if I had wanted to, until then I didn't believe the latter was possible. But there was more to this moment than simply sharing a ride in a car that was faster than his old Fury. Although we were father and son, we were both men, and somehow I felt as if I had finally measured up to the notch he had carved in some invisible yardstick many years earlier. I had not only risen to his expectation, but surpassed it. All of this took place as we approached the next traffic light and the 440 settled to a burbling idle.

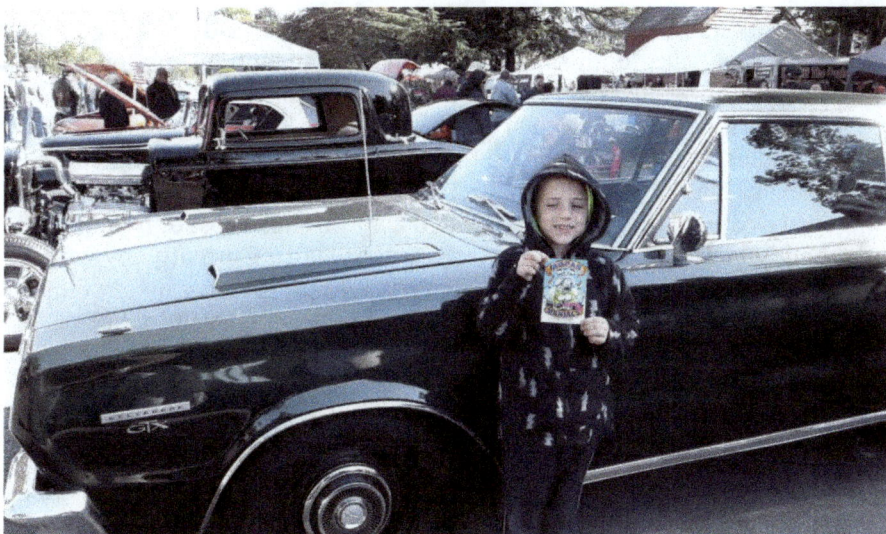

Linking Grandfathers and Grandsons

I often find myself wondering what caused us to become "car people." What caused the car bug to stir within us? Was it something that we were born with? Was it the result of a chain of events or experiences that took place early in our lives, during those years when we were most impressionable? Was it inspiration by a role model who was also infatuated with cars? Or, was it some combination of these factors? I also wonder if there was a certain moment in my life, a turning point that determined the course I would follow, and that cars would be at the epicenter of all that would come. Finally, how can we inspire future generations to appreciate the car hobby? How can we encourage them to cultivate their interest in automobiles?

My wife and I now have three grandchildren, all boys, ranging in age from newborn to seven. The older two are brothers who are inseparable. We take them to car shows and cruises a couple of times a year, but even though their experiences have been similar, their reactions to the cars are quite different. Michael, the older one, grows bored and fidgety. He seems to reach his saturation point within half an hour. Riley, who is now four, can't get enough. He asks me to pick him up so he can see the engines and interiors of nearly every car we see. He is enamored by the shapes of the bodies, the glisten of the wheels, gauges, and other ancillary add-ons, and the sanitary engine compartments. Although he cannot comprehend all that he is looking at, he understands enough to know that he loves it!

Thinking back to my earliest years, my parents had a '51 Ford with a flathead six and a column-shifted three-speed manual transmission with and electrically operated overdrive. Unfortunately, the Ford met its demise one night in 1971 when I was just six. As a toddler I had a toy Ford with a detailed underside, and as I learned to talk my father saw to it that I could identify every part of its chassis.

My parents owned a 1964 Dodge Dart through most of my childhood, which probably explains my love of Darts. Currently my wife and I own six 1964 through 1968 Darts. When I was growing up my father liked cars, but he only worked on them out of necessity. Even so, he seemed to know every make and model from the '40s and '50s and he would identify any car from that era we spotted on the road. When I was twelve he purchased a 1963 Corvair that was to be a father-son project, but aside from keeping it running, little happened with it. Automotive restoration simply wasn't his thing. Over my objection he and my mother traded it in on a new Volkswagen Rabbit when I was fourteen.

In 1967 my grandfather purchased a new Plymouth Belvedere I four-door sedan with an AM radio, automatic transmission, and no other options. I vaguely remember taking a walk with him near my grandparents' home in Frederick, Maryland one evening in the fall of that year. This is among my earliest memories, for my second birthday had passed just a few months earlier. My grandparents lived in what I remember as an upscale apartment complex with lots of grass, trees, a covered bridge, and a three-sided community-shared parking garage. "Grad" had the space at the far-right end of the building and that's where I remember him parking the Belvedere. He passed away in January, 1968.

After his death my grandmother learned to drive. She was 65 at the time, and she returned to the dealership where they had bought the Plymouth. The salesman taught her how to drive it. She drove the Belvedere for the next twenty years, peering through its steering wheel, and never complaining about its manual steering or brakes. In 1969, she moved back to her hometown of Wilmington, Delaware.

As a child I loved the lines of the Plymouth, the layout of its dash, and the styling of its one-year-only dog dish hubcaps. By the time I reached driving age in 1981 I had already come to appreciate its low mileage, great condition, and originality. "Gram" hung up the keys for good in 1988 at the age of 85. Three years later she gave the car to my father, and I acquired it from him in 1992. Aside from the one year that my father owned it, the Plymouth has spent its entire life sheltered from the elements.

No doubt, the presence of this Belvedere throughout my childhood and the happy memories associated with it sparked my love of its high-performance sister, the 1967 Belvedere GTX. My grandfather had been a very practical man, as evidenced by the short list of options he'd selected for the Belvedere. He was neither a car enthusiast nor a high-performance junkie, but if he had been, he might have chosen a GTX, and it's likely he would have optioned it similarly. Last November my wife and I acquired a low option GTX. It was originally equipped with the base 440 Super Commando engine, standard-issue column shifted Torque flite automatic transmission (the available four-speed was an extra-cost option), basic steel wheels, manual steering, manual drum brakes, and an AM radio. With so few check boxes having been selected on its order form, on some level I feel that this car pays homage to my grandfather. Its condition is less than perfect, but it was priced within our reach.

For the next month I worked to correct a number of minor issues in preparation to have it inspected and registered in Delaware. It is now legal and road worthy, and my focus has shifted to acquiring the parts necessary to address its cosmetic faults.

A few weeks before Christmas we kept Michael and Riley for the weekend. Among the activities we had planned was a Saturday night visit to the Festival of Lights in Ocean City, Maryland, an annual tradition for us. We returned home late that night and promptly put the boys to bed. Early Sunday morning I was heading out to the garage alone to work on the GTX for an hour or two before breakfast while my wife and the boys slept, but Riley had other ideas. He was wide awake and wanted to go to the garage with me. Reluctantly I agreed. I encourage the boys to come to the garage, but only when I can give them my full attention and supervision, not while I'm working.

As I fiddled with the choke on the GTX Riley scaled the oddly spaced steps leading to the loft. I warned him not to touch anything, to which he replied, "I'm not, gampop." Nothing crashed to the floor, so I left him alone to take in the sights of fenders, doors, dashboards, seats, and steering wheels. Sometime later he came downstairs and wandered about the cars that lay dormant under their covers. Then he stood back and watched me work. He appeared awe-struck, studying the car and me for quite some time without uttering a word. I sensed in him the same feeling I remember having years ago while straddling my bike on the sidewalk of our suburban community and watching the neighbors work on their cars in their driveways. I pretended not to notice Riley, for I didn't want to interrupt his thoughts as he processed all that he was seeing. Instead, I let him savor the moment. Furthermore, I wanted to show him that I trusted him to follow garage etiquette and not tamper with things. He did not disappoint me.

Finally, he approached the GTX. He studied the lines in the grille up close, then raised his arm and polished the headlights with his sleeve. When he was finished he gave the fender an affectionate pat.

And so it is that another 1967 Plymouth provides a link between a grandfather and his grandson. It's too early to say, but one day Riley might be the keeper of his grandfather's GTX.

Moose Finds His Way Home

On a sunny day in 2007 I was driving south toward Georgetown, Delaware on Route 113. Daisey's Used Cars was just ahead on the right, and I always made it a point to check out the cars on their lot. Charles Daisey, the owner, was a classic car enthusiast. In addition to the modern cars and trucks that filled the majority of his lot, he also dealt in classic and antique vehicles. These were the cars that piqued my interest, and on this day, I spied a white '68 Plymouth Road Runner with a blue interior.

Although I appreciated Road Runners, I had never aspired to own one. I had always gravitated to the smaller cars, but there was something about this car that spoke to me. More than likely, it was the color combination, for my parents had owned a white '69 Plymouth Fury with a blue interior from the time I was six until I was eleven.

A couple of days later, my wife, Kristan, spotted the Road Runner. Although she is also a car enthusiast, she had never voiced a desire to own an early Road Runner. It came as a surprise when, over dinner that evening, she told me about the amazing white Road Runner that she had seen on Daisey's lot, and that she wanted us to talk to Mr. Daisey to see if we could purchase it.

I stopped to see Mr. Daisey, and the price was a firm 19,000 dollars. Kristan had just been laid off, so unless we could work some magic, it would stay right where it was. While I was there, I looked it over thoroughly. The quarter panels had been replaced, most likely due to rust. The interior was in presentable condition, but it needed new carpet and a new headliner. The front bench seat had obviously been recovered, but the new fabric was just like the original. The rear seat appeared to be original, with the exception of the piece of vinyl at the top edge of the rear seat. A new piece of vinyl had been stitched in, but the shade of blue was not a perfect match. The chrome on the rear bumper was thin in places, the taillight bezels and door handles were lightly pitted, and the edges of the windshield had been fogged by age and moisture. I also saw evidence where it had been hit in the left front corner, although the fender had been replaced prior to the repaint. The frame rails, floor, and other body panels were solid. Despite its minor shortcomings, it appeared to be a good car.

Kristan had a '65 Mustang convertible which we had bought several years earlier. The original engine and transmission were long absent before we purchased it, so I built a 302 V-8 and I installed a four-speed manual transmission in place of its original automatic transmission. The quarter panels on the Mustang had been replaced too, and its paint looked like a low budget job. It was far from a show car, but it was a good fair-weather driver. She loved her Mustang, but much to my surprise, she was willing to sacrifice it for this Road Runner! We took it to Mr. Daisey to see what he would offer us in trade. I was less than optimistic, and for good reason. He made what I thought was a fair offer, but we were 5500 dollars apart. Short of borrowing money, we had no way to close the gap.

When we got back into the Mustang, I started the engine, pressed the clutch pedal, and moved the shifter into reverse. I heard a light clunk, and then the shifter felt loose in my hand. Peering under the car, I saw one end of the reverse shift rod lying on the ground. I walked back into Mr. Daisey's office and said, "You aren't going to believe this!" I told him what had happened, and he brought out his floor jack.

We raised the car enough for me to slither underneath and reattach the shifter linkage. I thanked him, and I stated that nothing like that had ever happened with that car before. I couldn't believe it had happened there, of all places. He winked and said, "They know."

While the car was on Daisey's lot, it wore three different wheel and tire combinations—steel wheels painted body color with the one year only Plymouth hubcaps, Magnum 500 wheels (called "Road Wheels" in Chrysler parlance), and American Racing Torq Thrust wheels with raised white letter tires. Kristan still lusted for the car, but even though we couldn't put it into our garage, we rationalized that we would see it around at local car shows. We were wrong. When it was sold, it vanished. We thought about the car often and we talked about it from time to time over the next few years, but we didn't see it at any area events, nor did any of our friends.

Not long after the Road Runner was sold, Kristy found work as a cook in a state-run facility south of Georgetown. Her daily commute took her past Daisey's lot. I had been a high school teacher, but in 2011 I accepted a job teaching at a northern campus of the state-run community college. One morning that November I was rushing out of my office and heading for class when the phone rang. Something told me to answer it, and immediately I recognized Kristan's voice. All she said was, "It's baa-ack!" Right away I knew she was talking about the Road Runner. Although we were in a better place financially, the timing was terrible, for we had just purchased our second rental house. It had been a foreclosure sold through an online auction, and despite the series of photos, we knew nothing about the condition of the major systems in the house.

I spent most of my winter break checking these systems and making minor repairs to the house. By early January, I felt much more confident about its overall condition. Without Kristan's knowledge, on Martin Luther King Day, I returned to Daisey's. The condition of the Road Runner had changed somewhat. The interim owner had replicated the optional factory black-out treatment in the center of the hood, but he had done so poorly, for there were deep scratches under the matte black paint. In addition, the factory cast iron intake manifold had been removed, and in its place was a purple painted Edelbrock Performer manifold. I found the original manifold on the floor behind the driver's seat. Mr. Daisey handed me the keys, and on the short road test I discovered that the steering wheel was ninety degrees off-center when driving straight, there was a shimmy in the front end at highway speeds, there was an objectionable brake pulsation, and the engine ran poorly, most likely due to improper timing and carburetor issues. The good news was that there were no strange noises, exhaust smoke, or anything that would indicate major mechanical trouble brewing.

The asking price was the same as it had been before, but this time I was able to negotiate it down a few thousand dollars. I left a small deposit, and I agreed to pick it up one evening later that week.

On that day, I left work early and I drove straight to Daisey's lot. My plan was to pick up the Road Runner and then surprise Kristan as she was leaving work. In late day traffic, I arrived later than I'd planned, and I simply didn't have enough time. While Mr. Daisey was completing the paperwork, I called Kristan and suggested that we meet for dinner at a restaurant in Georgetown. She agreed. When the paperwork was finished, Mr. Daisey affixed a temporary tag to the rear bumper, and per my request, he moved the car to the back of the lot.

I met Kristan for dinner. We exchanged talk about our day, and when the conversation fell into a lull, I said, "Hey, while we're both here in Georgetown, lets run over to Daisey's and look at that Road Runner."

She said, "Why? We can't buy it."

I said, "I just want to look at it again, together, and make sure we are both seeing the same things." She reluctantly agreed. Mr. Daisey had closed for the day by the time we arrived.

When she didn't see the car in its usual spot, Kristan exclaimed, "It's gone!"

I looked toward the back of the lot and said, "There it is."

We walked to the car, and slowly she circled it, her face bearing the look of longing. When she spotted the temporary tag she said, "Oh no! Somebody bought it!" I took her hand and placed the keys in it. "What's this?" she asked in disbelief.

"The keys," I said.

"For what?" I took the keys from her, unlocked the door, then sat inside and started the engine. She said, "You didn't really buy it. You're just working on it!"

I said, "No, it's yours." She hugged me tightly as she cried with delight.

With the gas gauge reading empty, we stopped for fuel on the way home. I filled the tank, and then I discovered a leak at the fuel gauge sender. After a few miles, once the engine was warm, I could smell oil burning off the exhaust manifolds due to leaking valve cover gaskets.

While completing the paperwork at Daisey's I learned that he had sold it to a man in Virginia previously. That explained why we hadn't seen it in our area during the interim.

In the days that followed, I installed the original intake manifold, replaced the valve cover gaskets, and installed a new fuel gauge sending unit. The replacement sender corrected the fuel leak, but its poor calibration rendered the gas gauge inaccurate. I sealed up the original sender with epoxy and reinstalled it. Over the next couple of months, I obtained an Edelbrock 750 CFM carburetor, and I used parts from a junk carburetor in order to mate it to the factory choke. I also replaced the rear main seal, outer door handles, and taillight bezels. Finally, I aligned the front suspension, recurved the distributor, resurfaced the brake drums, and balanced the wheels.

In addition to the accident damage to the left front and the mismatched vinyl on the rear seat, I discovered other peculiarities. An old electric fuel pump resided near the gas tank. It had been wired with small gauge wire that had been strung haphazardly along the underside of the car, although the wiring had long been disconnected. Of course, I had no way to know when the pump had been installed, but the pump and wiring both appeared to be too old to have been installed by the Virginia owner. I wondered, who would have done that to this car? In addition, there had been traction bars installed at one time. Rather than remove them and reinstall the lower shock absorber plates, someone had merely torched the traction bars off, leaving their mounting plates in place.

We drive our cars long distances, often on interstates at high speeds. I refuse to have a car that can't keep up with today's traffic comfortably, for such a car is not only nerve-wracking to drive, it is also dangerous. To that end, I removed the 3.23:1 ratio ring and pinion from the rear axle. In their place, I installed a 2.76 ring and pinion along with a Sure-Grip differential.

On a crisp evening in early March, I took the car for a road test while tuning the carburetor. On a relatively straight secondary road, I floored the accelerator from a slow roll, and I stayed at full throttle through first gear, second gear, and into third gear before lifting my foot. I made several of these twenty-to-one hundred mile per hour blasts, for there was not another soul on the road. The car felt great! But suddenly, headlights appeared quite some distance behind me. I had not passed anybody pulling out of a driveway or side road, so I didn't know where this vehicle had come from. There were no flashing lights, but still....

Ahead, the road entered a small wood and it curved to the right. I had gone far enough anyway, so at the end of the curve I made a U-turn and started heading back toward home. As I rounded the curve and exited the woods, I was greeted by a state police vehicle that was moving about as fast as I had been moments earlier. After we passed, he continued at a high rate of speed in pursuit of his speeder, not realizing that his speeder was me. I kissed my hand and patted the dashboard. The Road Runner was now a part of our family!

Kristan enjoyed driving her Road Runner, and she named it Moose. Though not a traditional name for such a car, she reasoned that it was big and powerful just like a moose. It hinted at our love of Maine, which has a large moose population.

Mr. Daisey had contracted with a local body shop to repaint Moose shortly after he had acquired it in 1997. We contacted the same body shop about having the hood repainted. Kristan drove it there one afternoon after work. Two men removed the hood, and she drove the car home. After the paint work had been completed a few days later, she drove it back to the body shop and the guys reinstalled and aligned the hood. We also had a local upholstery shop replace the headliner and carpet, and we had them sublet the replacement of the windshield. Over the following years, I replaced the Torq Thrust wheels and aging tires with factory fifteen-inch steel wheels, the correct hubcaps, and new tires. I also replaced the rear bumper.

We knew nearly nothing about Moose's history, but that didn't stop us from enjoying the car often. We attended numerous local shows, cruised in Ocean City, Maryland, and attended a couple of Northeast Hemi Owners Association club meets. I use Facebook as a communication tool, and I have found it valuable for locating parts and obtaining information for our cars. Over the years, I had posted pictures of our cars in various groups, and folks usually "liked" or left positive comments.

One day in 2018, I received a message from a gentleman named Scott Smith. He said, "I think you might have my old car." I asked him what he could tell me about it that would identify it as his. Rather than tell me about unique characteristics, he provided me the VIN of the car he once owned. It matched our car.

Over the next couple of days, he wrote several installments in Facebook Messenger filling in much of the Road Runner's history dating all the way back to 1975. Scott is an Ohio native, and the paperwork he'd found in the glove compartment indicated that the Road Runner had been sold new at Bill Swad Chrysler-Plymouth near his hometown.

In 1981, when he was fourteen, he and his father went to a local junkyard to purchase parts for a car they were working on. While his dad spoke to the older gentleman who owned the yard, Scott spotted a car hiding under a tarpaulin. He lifted a corner of the tarp and discovered a white Road Runner. He called his father over, and his father then inquired about it. The proprietor stated that the car had come into the yard in 1975 following an accident in which the left front corner was damaged. Rather than part it out and scrap it, he had set it aside and covered it with the tarp to ensure that it stayed intact. He had planned to repair it, but he hadn't yet gotten to it. Scott's father negotiated with the salvage yard owner, and he wound up with the car in exchange for painting a Pinto station wagon.

By the time Scott turned sixteen, he and his father had replaced the damaged fender and front bumper, and Scott drove the Road Runner while he was in high school. "I worked for almost an entire summer to save up enough money for the front seat upholstery," Scott said, "but I didn't have enough for the back seat." A family friend had replaced the sunbaked upper portion of the rear seat vinyl with a new piece that was close to the factory color.

After a few years he sold it in order to buy a very clean and original '73 Road Runner, but the deal fell through. He was able to buy his '68 Road Runner back a couple of years later. Over time a hot 440 found its way under the hood and new quarter panels replaced the rusty originals. The over-assisted power steering gave way to manual steering. By then it had long been retired from daily use, and it served him as a fun fair-weather cruiser that regularly clicked off twelve second passes at the local dragstrip.

Eventually, Scott married, and soon he had two sons. In their early years, they often rode in the Road Runner with their Dad. Unfortunately, in 2007 Scott and his wife divorced. He yanked the hot 440 and installed a 400 in its place using the external bolt-on pieces from the original 383. He then sold his prized Road Runner to someone who flipped it. It wound up going through the auto auction in Harrisburg, Pennsylvania. From there it went to Daisey's Used Cars in Georgetown, Delaware.

Scott was relieved to know where his Road Runner was. He had tracked it down while it was in Virginia, but he didn't know where it had gone from there. He said he'd love to buy it back one day if it ever came up for sale, but he also wanted to provide as much history as possible to the current owners.

Suddenly, so much of what I'd discovered about the car made sense. The fuel pump had been wired up by a high schooler. Yes, the car had been raced. And that accident damage? Because it had sidelined the 'Runner in 1975 while, presumably, it was still being driven daily during Ohio's harsh winters, that may be the only reason why the car had survived at all.

I was thankful to Scott for reaching out to me. Since becoming friends with him, I have gained a new appreciation for the Road Runner. Suddenly, it became more than just a pretty white car. It has an identity, and its story makes it unique. It is our cars' stories that lend them their individuality.

I assured Scott that we would honor his request. If we ever decided to sell it, we would offer it to him first. Kristan and I both felt that we would like for him to have his car back one day.

In early 2019, Scott came across a deal on a mostly original bright red '73 Road Runner. It had low mileage, its interior was in good condition, and its original 340 cubic inch engine and automatic transmission were still in place. He asked me, "Do you think Kristan would want to trade?"

I said, "I don't know. You'll have to run it by her." I didn't think there was any chance she would be willing to do the trade, but she surprised me by entertaining the thought. She said she had always been fond of the "Daisy Duke style" Road Runners. We took a weekend trip to Ohio to meet Scott and his wife Felicia and to see the '73 Road Runner. Kristy and I both drove it, and although the steering seemed very twitchy, it ran and drove fine otherwise. I figured that aligning the front suspension and adjusting the power steering box would cure it. We discussed some body issues that needed to be addressed, and we agreed that once they were done, we would trade cars. It was a gentlemen's agreement, sealed with nothing more than a handshake.

Over the next year, we stayed in close contact with Scott while his work on the '73 Road Runner progressed. He made the body repairs as discussed, and he also installed new carpet and addressed the cracked dash pad. Over and over, he said, "I just want you guys to be happy." Of course, getting his old Road Runner back would surely make him happy.

We agreed to meet in Cumberland, Maryland on a weekend late in the spring of 2020. Cumberland is roughly the half-way point between our homes. Kristan and I trailered Moose from our home in Delaware to our meeting place in Cumberland a day ahead of time. Scott and Felicia trailered the '73 Road Runner from their home in Ohio. In the motel parking lot, we unloaded our cars and made the trade. We exchanged keys, signed paperwork, and took photos. Then we each loaded our respective cars onto our trailers. After lunch in a nearby restaurant, we parted ways and headed for our respective homes.

Kristan had already picked the name Scarlet for her new Road Runner. Moments after I unloaded it in our driveway, she went for a blast down our road. I have spent some time sorting out some of the minor issues that are typical with old cars, and we enjoy driving it just as we did Moose.

Shortly after taking possession of Moose, Scott accepted a job as the shop manager of a classic car dealership and repair shop. Through his connections there, he acquired a complete 426 Hemi engine. He has since rebuilt the Hemi and installed it into Moose, along with all of the correct emblems, air cleaner, and other details that make it appear as though it had been installed at the factory more than half a century earlier.

Although the first seven years of the car's existence had been a mystery since Scott first discovered the '68 Road Runner in the junkyard, he had found what appeared to be the original owner's name in the paperwork in the glovebox. Over the years, all of his attempts to locate the original owner led to dead ends. Through some of his connections made in recent years, he discovered that the original owner was Mark Campbell, who worked for Jeg Coughlin, both as a machinist and as a member of his race team. Eventually Mark left to start his own machine shop. Later, he raced a top fuel dragster under the moniker Roach Coach, achieving notoriety in the late 1970s and early 1980s. Unfortunately, he is now deceased. Scott has spoken to one of Mark's friends who claims that Mark had purchased the Road Runner to use as his daily transportation, not to race. He sold it sometime in the early 1970s. Owner number two remains a mystery. At the time of the collision, it was a seven-year-old car that was presumably not worth fixing, so it was sent to the junkyard.

It is satisfying when a story comes full-circle, and the tale of Scott's Road Runner has certainly done that. Kristan and I are happy to see that the car is now back home where it belongs, and we are glad to have been able to help make that happen, but we are also happy with the car we got in exchange. We know Scott appreciates our willingness to return his car to him, but we appreciate his willingness to make the '73 as nice as he did.

My Blue Mistress

It was late on a Saturday afternoon when my Uncle Richard's tan Dodge Tradesman work van pulled into the dirt driveway that encircled my grandparents' house near Mardela Springs, Maryland. Tall and slender, Uncle Richard stepped from his truck and spotted me near the side door of Grandpop's shop, which sat behind the house. "Hey Asbury, how's your hammer hanging?" he called to me. It was his standard greeting. He teased me, calling me by my middle name, because he knew that I hated it.

I ignored the Asbury comment and replied to his question with my standard answer, "Straight up."

"You're a damned liar!" he said with a grin. I wasted no time in retrieving my bag of clothes from inside the house and saying good-bye to my parents and grandparents before hopping into the van with Uncle Richard.

My grandfather, William Adkins, had gone into business as a carpenter in 1953. My father, his older brother Uncle Richard, and his younger brother Uncle Ernest had all worked for him through their teenage years. My father and Uncle Ernest had moved on to pursue other interests, but Uncle Richard had stayed with the business. Most of their jobs were in the Salisbury, Maryland area. Since Grandpop's heart attack a year earlier, Uncle Richard had worked alone.

For many summers, I had spent a week or two with my grandparents. During these weeks, I had gone to work with Grandpop and

Uncle Richard every day. There, I usually performed menial tasks such as cleaning up and moving supplies, but sometimes I got to do "real" work, including nailing on roof sheathing and shingles. My older cousins, Richard Jr. and David, were usually on the job as well. Although they had grown up in the business like their father, by the time they reached adulthood they had both moved on to other ventures. I was very close with both Grandpop and Uncle Richard.

My parents, my two younger sisters, and I visited Grandmom and Grandpop a few times a year. We would drive the 100 miles from our home near Wilmington, Delaware on Friday night or early Saturday morning, and we would return on Sunday afternoon. The ritual always included attending church, which I despised. It wasn't that I didn't believe in God, for I most certainly did. The problem was that my family's church believed in absolute predestination. Those who were destined for Heaven had been pre-selected by God before the beginning of time. Jesus had died for his people, but if I wasn't one of those fortunate few, then my fate was sealed; I was bound for hell along with the masses. To me, it seemed that salvation was doled out in a manner similar to lottery winnings, and I found this unsettling. When I was younger, I had often laid awake in bed fretting over where I would spend eternity. Consequently, church was a place where I found more fear than comfort, so I didn't care to attend. By the paradox of absolute predestination, I reasoned that if I was one of His children, I didn't need to go, for I already had a free pass into Heaven. And if I wasn't one of His, then I still didn't need to go, for my attendance wouldn't change anything anyway. Uncle Richard knew of my feeling toward church, so he would often ask if I could help him with some task on Saturday night or early Sunday morning. He would pick me up, and I would stay with Aunt Linda and him.

On one such Sunday outing sometime in the mid-1970s, we went clamming at the southern end of Assateague Island, just offshore from Chincoteague, Virginia. Uncle Richard had placed a large round basket inside an inflated inner tube from a truck, which he tied to his waist with a short length of rope. We walked into the water, each carrying a clamming rake which had tines shaped much like the toes of a sloth. He said we would feel for the clams with our feet, then scoop them up quickly with the rake before they could burrow deep into the sand. "Watch for jellyfish," he warned.

The water was at midriff level for Uncle Richard, but it came up to my neck. With the glare from the sun on the surface of the murky water, I could only see the jellyfish that were close to the surface. Soon, I experienced an excruciating burning sensation across my thighs. Then my left foot. Then my right arm. It was clear that Uncle Richard hadn't anticipated the sheer number of these translucent floating gobs of snot with long, stinging tentacles that, whether by intent or happenstance, sought human flesh. He suggested that I go back to the car and wait, but I was determined to stick it out. I remember being amazed by how easily he retrieved clam after clam from the sand beneath our feet, and how fast he was filling the basket. I don't think I got more than one or two.

Suddenly, I spotted a jellyfish a few feet away drifting in the mild current, and I was directly in its path. I tried to move, but the deep water made it impossible to do so in time. It straddled me with its tentacles, some stretched across my chest and the remaining ones across my back. I don't remember how I escaped, but after that, I waited at the car.

Another of our outings took place in early January, 1979 when I was thirteen. We left his house early on Sunday morning and drove over icy roads to the Salisbury, Maryland airport to meet Uncle Ernest, who was an electronics wizard. He repaired office machines for IBM, and his territory included all of Delaware and the entire Delmarva Peninsula. He and Aunt Janie had just bought a tiny two-seat airplane, and he wanted to take me for a ride.

On this day, Uncle Richard and I drove my eldest cousin Becky's faded blue 1968 Dodge Dart GT. Bought new for Aunt Janie by Uncle Ernest in the fall of 1967, it had become Uncle Ernest's work car a few years later when they had bought a new Plymouth Satellite station wagon to better accommodate their growing family. I remember the Dart fondly, for it was always present at family gatherings. By 1977, the years of hauling Uncle Ernest's test equipment and tools from one job site to the next were showing, for the car was weathered and worn. Uncle Ernest had spoken of junking it, but Uncle Richard intervened. Together they replaced the leaking water pump and tuned it up, and then Uncle Richard had new tires installed. Despite its high mileage, it was still mechanically sound. Uncle Ernest then sold it to Becky for one dollar.

I don't remember what Uncle Richard and I talked about as we drove, but I do remember the exhaust note of the 273 cubic inch V-8 as he applied throttle judiciously on the slick roads. The Dart had a striking color combination—light blue paint with a black vinyl top and a two-tone interior. White bucket seats and door panels contrasted with blue carpet, seatbelts, headliner, dashboard, and the upper and lower metal trim of the doors. Uncle Richard didn't believe in seatbelts, but I wore mine.

Soon, Uncle Ernest and I climbed into his airplane. I was taken aback by the number of gauges, dials, and knobs that occupied the dashboard. I was also surprised to see controls on both sides of the cockpit. It amazed me that Uncle Ernest knew how to operate such a machine, and over the radio he spoke with the man in the control tower fluently in aviation jargon.

We taxied to the end of the runway where we stopped, waited for clearance, and then throttled up. As we gained speed, Uncle Ernest pulled the yoke toward him, and then we were airborne! He took me on an aerial tour of Salisbury, and he even flew west to circle above Grandmom and Grandpop's house before returning to the airport. Along the way, he asked me to take the controls on my side of the plane. Under his guidance, I gained and lost altitude, and I turned both left and right. It was amazing! Even now, as I watch the crop dusters performing their aerial acrobatics over the fields near our southern Delaware home, I think back to my flight with Uncle Ernest and I wonder if I missed my calling.

I have many other memories of the Dart. When I was about seven, I taunted Uncle Ernest by pretending that I was going to blow the horn. He showed me that if he twisted the horn button, it would come off. Then, he unplugged the black wire from what I would later learn was the horn switch. He reinstalled the horn button and said, "Go ahead and blow the horn." Of course, it didn't work. I don't know why I remember this, but half a century later it stands out as one of my most vivid childhood memories.

I also recall the July afternoon in 1979 when David, Richard Jr., and I were heading to my grandparents' in the Dart for Grandpop's birthday celebration. Richard was driving, and he wanted to stop by his girlfriend's house briefly even though we were already running late. He pressed the pedal hard despite David's warning of a heavy police presence on that particular road. Richard Jr. replied, "I don't have time for the cops!" While they argued, I sat in the back seat taking in Bad Company's Rock 'n' Roll Fantasy, which blared from the single speaker in the dashboard.

On a snowy Saturday in early 1981, David and I were driving around in his Dodge Charger when we came upon Becky, who was driving the Dart. We played cat and mouse for a while on the snow-covered roads of rural Wicomico County, east of Salisbury.

One night not long afterward, David and I were out clowning around in the Dart, and somebody began following us. David attempted to outrun our pursuant. He put enough space between us and the other car so that we lost sight momentarily—long enough to pull into somebody's driveway. He doused the lights until the other car passed. Only when we got a look at the other car did we realize that we had eluded a police officer. Moments later, every light inside and outside of the house came on. David rammed the shifter into Reverse, tore out of the gravel driveway in a hail of stones, and sped off in the direction from which we had come.

On this particular stay with Uncle Richard, which took place in November of 1982 during my senior year in high school, we would be working on Becky's Dart. A few months earlier, the timing chain had failed and several of the valves had been bent when they collided with the pistons. Uncle Richard had replaced the timing chain, and he had removed the cylinder heads to have the valves repaired by a local machine shop. He had reassembled the engine, but he could not coerce it to start. Together, we hoped to determine why. As far as I was concerned, it didn't matter what we found. Working on the Dart sure beat the hell out of going to church!

After breakfast the next morning, we connected a pair of jumper cables between the Dart and Uncle Richard's van. The starter cranked and cranked, but the engine showed no sign of life. We checked for spark, and although it wasn't as strong as we would have liked, we agreed that it was sufficient. We dribbled fuel down the throat of the carburetor, again to no avail. We removed and inspected the spark plugs, and we confirmed the firing order. We also made sure that the rotor was lined up with the tower for number one cylinder on the distributor cap when number one cylinder was at the top of the compression stroke. I had brought a few tools, among them a compression gauge. We checked the compression of a couple of cylinders, and we got readings of around 60 pounds per square inch, which was less than half of what the readings should have been. Either Uncle Richard had timed the engine wrong when he had installed the new timing chain, or the piston rings were so badly worn that the engine wouldn't run. Rather than invest more time and money into the car, he gave up. Sometime later he pushed it to a spot next to the garage under a pine tree.

My relationship with my father had been strained for a number of years, but it was now deteriorating rapidly. He insisted that I attend the University of Delaware even though none of their majors, nor the thought of college life as a whole, appealed to me. Cars were my passion, and I was determined to attend Automotive Training Center 35 miles away in Exton, Pennsylvania. Although this had become the greatest source of friction between us, we clashed over everything. I felt that in his eyes nothing I did was right; nothing I achieved was ever good enough. Consequently, I avoided him as much as possible. Things were easier that way.

My seventy mile daily round-trip commute meant that I would need a dependable and reasonably economical car. I had a 1964 Dart, which had belonged to my great aunt, and which I had purchased from my father when I was fifteen. I had swapped a three-speed manual transmission in place of its ailing automatic transmission before I was old enough to drive it. Unfortunately, it was titled in my father's name because I was a minor. Attempting to maintain control over me, he spoke often of selling it. I already knew that I would be paying my own way through automotive school, but now I also needed another car, one that couldn't be sold from under me. On New Year's Day when we were all together at Grandmom and Grandpop's I asked Uncle Richard about buying Becky's Dart. He replied that he would only sell it to me if my father approved. Of course, my father did not. A few weeks later, he told me, "That car is gone. I told Uncle Richard to get rid of it." I was devastated.

But soon I learned that the Dart wasn't gone. When we went to Uncle Richard and Aunt Linda's in February for my cousin David's wedding, it was still sitting beside their garage. Although I could not buy it directly, I was determined to make it mine, and so I devised a plan.

A few years earlier I had a morning newspaper route. One spring, I began mowing lawns for some of my customers, one of which was a man named Joe Arcuri. Joe owned a vacuum cleaner and sewing machine repair shop, and that summer he offered me a full-time job fixing vacuum cleaners. I was fifteen at the time, and I continued working for Joe until his death less than a year later. Some months prior to Joe's death, he and his wife, Theresa, hired Steve Gray, a former employee. Four years my senior, Steve and I became fast friends. After Joe's death, Theresa sold the business to a man named Bill Bush, and Bill was happy to keep Steve and me on staff.

Steve was well aware of my situation. I asked him if he would be willing to buy the Dart from Uncle Richard and then sell it to me after my 18th birthday. He agreed. We set a date for March 13th to pick it up, and we would drag it home behind my '64 Dart using a tow chain. I lined it up with Uncle Richard, and I also secured a place to store it, which was in a field behind John Reed's Garage, an old-time auto repair shop near my work and only a couple of miles from home. But on the beautiful sunny morning of March 13th, Steve was sick. I drove to Uncle Richard's alone hoping to pay for the car and get the title, which he would sign over to Steve. We would set another date to pick up the car.

When I arrived, I explained that Steve was sick and that I had nobody to steer the '68 Dart or to operate the brakes. Even so, Uncle Richard and I removed its driveshaft and we positioned it so that it was facing down the driveway. He asked who was really buying the car, and I insisted that Steve was. He said, "Frank, don't let me catch you in a lie."

I said, "Don't worry. You won't." Then I told him of my plans to swap in a six-cylinder engine and a manual transmission.

He said, "I thought this Steve guy was buying it."

I nodded. "He is." Uncle Richard shook his head. He didn't ask any more questions. It seemed that he already knew more than he wanted to. I didn't want to cause a rift between him and my father, but I would have felt guilty if I had withheld my intention from him. Although we never discussed it in the years that followed, I think he understood.

Then he said he had an idea. He procured four old tires which were not mounted on wheels. We sandwiched the tires between the rear bumper of my '64 Dart and the front bumper of the '68, and we chained the two cars together tightly. "You won't be able to make any sharp turns, but aside from that, you should be okay." In retrospect, why he thought this arrangement was satisfactory at all, much less for a 100-mile trip, is beyond me. But he was my Uncle Richard. Rather than question his judgement, I took his word that it would work, and it did. I handed over "Steve's" money—thirty dollars for the scrap value of the car, plus seventy dollars for the recapped tires that had been installed right before the timing chain had failed, in exchange for the title with Steve's name written in as the buyer.

The trip to Wilmington was slow, but mostly uneventful. Only twice did the '68 choose not to follow the '64, once at the end of Uncle Richard's driveway, and once when rounding a gentle curve at 50 MPH on Route 13 south of Smyrna. The latter incident gave me a moment of panic when I felt the aft end of the '64 Dart being yanked hard to the left, but then the '68 complied. I altered my route to avoid all tight turns, and I made it all but the last five miles before the tires shifted and one began dragging on the ground. Rather than stop, unchain the cars, and attempt to reposition the tires, I let it drag.

When I reached John Reed's place, I pulled into the field where the '68 Dart would remain during its rebirth, and then I unchained it from the '64 Dart.

It's not that I didn't love my '64 Dart. On the contrary, I did. I had spent countless hours working on it, repairing its rust and dings, and making it just the way I wanted it. It was equipped with an anemic 170 cubic inch Slant Six, but with the timing advanced several degrees it ran well. My only gripe about it was that it was a four-door, and I wanted a two-door. But with the ever-present danger that it would be sold, I decided to invest nothing more than absolutely necessary to keep it operable while devoting my remaining time and money to the '68.

The front end of the '64 was out of alignment, and soon the front tires were bald. I rotated them to the rear and put the good tires from the rear onto the front, figuring that this would buy me a little bit more time. It did until one stormy night that spring. I was on my way home from work with my buddy Mike Cullen following in his '64 Chevy pick-up when, on a right-hand bend, the rear of the '64 Dart began to hydroplane. The tail came around to the left, and despite counter-steering, I could not straighten it. It continued its spin—sideways, backwards, and beyond. The right rear wheel struck the curb on the right side of the road, at which point the front end swung violently to the right and also collided with the hard concrete. The car ground to a sparky halt on the sidewalk. Two tires were flat, three of the four wheels were bent, and the front wheels were oriented in a manner never intended by the factory. I had it towed home, and although I could have fixed it, it would have been far more work and expense than I was able to invest at that time. And for what? A car that I was only going to lose anyway? Instead, I pulled the engine and transmission for use in the '68. From the outset I had said that the '68 would have a Slant Six and a manual transmission, but I hadn't planned to source those parts from my '64.

The months that followed were incredibly busy. I formulated a plan for how I wanted to build the Dart, and I started acquiring parts. When the week of Easter break came around, I removed the automatic transmission and dragged it out of the way. I didn't have a jack to lower it, so I had to unbolt it and let it fall. The muddy ground cushioned its landing. I also removed the steering column and power steering box, replacing them with the manual steering parts from the '64 Dart. Finally, I removed the air conditioning that Uncle Ernest had added when the Dart was new. During that week, I scored numerous junkyard finds, including a black carpet set that was in better condition than the tattered blue original carpet.

When Mike and I pulled the lifeless 273 V-8, I could not afford to rent an engine hoist. I removed the hood, and we pushed the car close to the only nearby tree. The first branch of that tree was fifteen feet from the ground, and my ratcheting come along had only ten feet of cable. We used a tow chain to make up the difference. I shinnied up the tree and affixed the come along to the branch. Then we connected the hook on the cable to the tow chain, and I bolted the chain to two of the carburetor studs on the intake manifold. Because we couldn't center the car under the branch, the chain and cable were not quite vertical, which meant that the engine would not rise straight upward. I climbed back up the tree to operate the come along while Mike stood on the inner fenders and guided the engine out with a shovel. One of the carburetor studs snapped when the engine was about a foot off the frame, but fortunately the other one held. When the engine was high enough to clear the front of the car, we shoved the Dart back into its spot and we lowered the engine into the bed of the truck.

After our experience with removing the 273, I saved enough money to rent an engine hoist to install the Slant Six. On a Saturday morning, I went to ABC Rental, picked up the pieces of the hoist, and took them to John Reed's place. I pushed the car to a spot where the ground was flat, and I lowered the engine into place. All went well until I pushed it back to its original spot. I could only turn the steering wheel one revolution in each direction before the steering linkage hit the oil pan! The '64 and '68 Darts were different body styles, but I didn't realize just how different they were structurally. It was immediately obvious that the '64 oil pan was not compatible with the '68 chassis. I found the correct oil pan on a junk engine in a large pile of dead engines at a local junkyard, but I couldn't afford to rent the hoist a second time. Instead, I found a four-by-four of an appropriate length. I laid it across the engine compartment and chained it to the engine. Then I used a long two-by-four and pried up one side of the four-by-four. I placed a brick under it. Then I pried up the other side of the four-by-four and placed two bricks under it. Working back and forth see-sawing the four-by-four, I raised the engine high enough from the frame to remove the oil pan. It was tedious, but effective.

Mike had a 1965 Plymouth Belvedere with a bad transmission. I bought it for parts and to use as a shed, and I parked it next to the Dart. Not many of the parts from the Belvedere would fit the Dart, but it was handy for small things. It was also nice to be able to store my tools and parts securely.

Over the next couple of months, I installed the manual transmission, hacked the required holes in the floor for the shifter and linkage with a hammer and chisel, and fashioned a floor hump from the steel casing of an old canister-style vacuum cleaner. I also rebuilt the front suspension.

By the time I graduated high school, the Dart was operable, though not legally. Uncle Richard came up for my graduation, and he wanted to see the progress I had made. After the graduation ceremony, we drove to John Reed's place. I fired up the Dart and drove it around the field. There were no front seats in it then, for I had removed them so that the torn coverings could be repaired. Instead, I sat on a cinder block which I had found nearby. He was almost as thrilled as I was!

With high school and most of the mechanical work on the Dart now behind me, my focus shifted to refurbishing the interior and repairing the body. By now, I was working full-time for the summer, and I was also on my own, renting a room from Steve and his wife in the basement of the house that they rented. Coincidentally, this house was only a block from John Reed's place, so on nice evenings I often drove the Dart to Steve's house and worked on it there. That was especially convenient after I had completed the body work and began wet sanding the old blue paint. I parked in the yard and trickled water from a hose onto the body panels while I sanded. Def Leppard's Pyromania had come out a couple of months earlier, and I would often place one of my stereo speakers in the basement window so I could listen to music while I worked.

Regarding the body work, I'd had no training whatsoever. What little I knew, I had picked up on my own beginning when I was fifteen. I covered most of the rust holes in the lower extremities with sheet aluminum, pop-riveted to the original metal under the molding that ran the length of the car. I filled minor dings with Bondo brand body filler, sanded smooth with 80 grit, followed by finer grit sandpapers. For the amateur job that it was, it looked surprisingly good. In late July, K and H Auto Body repainted the Dart in its original light blue hue, and I added a set of Rally wheels from a Plymouth Duster. I also had a local shop align the front end.

Soon it was August. My eighteenth birthday fell on a Saturday, so on the following Monday afternoon, Steve and I went to the nearby Department of Motor Vehicle. The Dart passed inspection on the first try. Steve had a title issued in his name, and he promptly signed it over to me. I got back into the Title line, and minutes later I was issued a title in my name.

As much as I had healed my Dart, it had healed me too. The last two years of high school had been a long period of misery during which I knew I was biding my time. Even now, spring of my junior year stands out as the lowest point in my life for the simple reason that I could not see a way out of my situation. Therefore, I held no hope. By the time I began my senior year, I had things somewhat figured out. I also dated briefly during this time—no small feat for a socially awkward introvert who had harbored an inferiority complex for much of his life. Although I couldn't see it at the time, I expected far too much of that relationship. I disclosed little about my situation, for I was desperate to find a counterbalance to the negativity. I was grasping for something positive, and I was sure that I had found it. I clung to it, and in so doing, I smothered it.

Regarding that nagging inferiority complex, it is what drove me to spend countless hours tinkering with mechanical things as a child, thus developing my mechanical skill. From bicycles to lawn mowers, to a go-kart, and finally to cars, I had taken a logical and evolutionary path during which I had learned all that I could from each step. By the time I was eight years old, mechanics had become my identity, and it was an identity that I was proud of. Early-on, I had believed that I could build a life on mechanics. And soon, I would.

My automotive education began at Automotive Training Center a few weeks later. For the next year, I continued working at Bill's Sew and Vac. I also compiled a list of minor issues with the Dart, and I eradicated all of them, although I was still learning to manage my living expenses. Only once did I make the mistake of grocery shopping while I was hungry. I had my budget cut slim to the point that for a while, I could only afford to eat dinner every-other night. Even then, it was something from a can—lots of Chef Boyardee and mac 'n' cheese. There was no stove in the basement at Steve's, but I had the use of a refrigerator and a sink, and I had my own hot plate. Once every week or two, I treated myself to a couple of McDonald's cheeseburgers. I slept on a cot, and I had access to the washer and dryer. Soon, Mike was living there too.

What I hadn't expected were the unplanned expenses—auto parts for minor repairs, mainly. Once school got underway, while the Dart proved reliable, there were problems that arose from time to time. I solved some of the reoccurring ignition troubles by retrofitting electronic ignition using pieces claimed from a few junk cars at East Seventh Street Auto Salvage in Wilmington. Using a wiring diagram from a service manual for a later car, I connected the new ignition components in the Sew and Vac parking lot well after hours on a Saturday night.

The battery was the old one from my wrecked '64 Dart, and it began to fail. Steve's house sat on a corner lot, and the side street was on a slight hill. I parked there so that in the morning, I could start the engine without using the starter. I would coast to build a little bit of speed, slip the transmission into second gear, turn on the ignition, and engage the clutch. With a lurch, the engine came to life. At school, I tried to get a parking space on an incline, but if I was unable to, I would push the car to a sloped portion of the lot and start it the same way. It was two weeks before I could afford to buy a new battery.

As the miles rolled up on the odometer over the first couple of months, the engine began consuming oil at an alarming rate. Under John Reed's tutelage, I replaced the valve guide seals, but the new seals did little to curb the Dart's appetite for oil. It became clear that the current engine would not last for the duration of my time in school. I removed the engine from Mike's old Belvedere, which was a 225 cubic inch Slant Six. It, too, was tired, so I hauled it to school for a rebuild. Enlisting the help of the machine shop students, the cylinders were bored oversize and the crankshaft journals were turned undersize. Since I was rebuilding it, I took the opportunity to install a hotter camshaft in an effort to increase the power output of the six cylinder. On a cold February day, I swapped the engine, along with a four-speed manual transmission, into the Dart. I was forced to dip heavily into my savings, which put me onto a collision course with bankruptcy.

Compounding matters, I needed front tires, but I had no budget for them. One afternoon while on my way from school to work, I lost traction on a snowy curve and rammed a stout tree. It was a low-speed impact, but it damaged the hood, fender, grille, and bumper. With no other choice, I applied for a Sears credit card, and I used it to buy front tires. Making minimum payments, I was still paying off those tires long after I had used them up.

The new 225 ran well, but my quest for speed was heating up. Not long after I installed it, I modified a spare one-barrel intake manifold so that it would accept a larger two-barrel carburetor. I had a lot to learn about carburetor tuning, but I reasoned that there was no better way to learn than by tuning my own car for both power and fuel economy. By the time I graduated, I had replaced that manifold with an Offenhauser four-barrel manifold and a 600 CFM Holley vacuum secondary carburetor. I had also replaced the stock exhaust system with a pair of Clifford long tube headers and cobbled dual exhaust. Again, carburetor tuning proved challenging, but the end result was a car that could run with most stock small block V-8s while achieving upward of 20 MPG. According to the ancient chassis dynamometer at school, I had doubled the horsepower of the Slant Six.

Of course, I engaged in automotive hijinks whenever possible. I competed in countless stoplight drag races, and I became interested in handling on the hilly and curvy two-lane secondary roads of northern Delaware and southeastern Pennsylvania. For a while, I carpooled with three other students. Our route took us on a road with a railroad crossing that had a steep approach on one side and a gentle fall on the other. I discovered that 53 miles per hour was the optimum speed. At any lower speed, the rear wheels would catch the track on the far side of the crossing. At a higher speed, the car would soar too far before contacting the road, leading to a hard landing. At 53 miles per hour, it wasn't obvious that the car had left the ground, but the railroad tracks seemed to disappear from beneath the tires.

For my second year of school, I was forced to take out a student loan, but I stayed on course, and I graduated in the spring of 1985. Along the way, I changed jobs, first working for a tire retail chain doing alignments, and then for a small independent repair shop doing everything except for alignments. After graduation, I moved to another friend's basement in Claymont, Delaware.

The two years of automotive school had been hard on the Dart. A number of minor traffic incidents, most of them not my fault, had left the body somewhat battered. Rust had begun to reappear in a couple of places, the vinyl top was coming apart, and a fellow student had clobbered the left fender in the parking lot while doing donuts in the snow in his Pinto. Upon graduation, I started working long hours, often clocking as many as twenty hours a day. I treated the Dart to a new set of radial tires and a budget paintjob, and I also had a new dual exhaust system fabricated. Eventually, I replaced the white seats and door panels with black pieces from a parts car that I had acquired. By summertime, the Dart was looking good again, but the shop I had been working for had gone out of business. I took another job, which soon led to another, and another. In the spring of 1986, I bought a rusty '66 Dodge D-100 pick-up, so the Dart was spared salted winter roads from that point forward.

It was not my intention to keep the Dart forever. I expected the body to eventually rust away to the point that the car could no longer be saved. I thought I would be forced to let it go eventually, but I could never envision that day. I vowed to preserve it so that my time with it would be as long as possible.

From a financial standpoint, my first few years in the automotive field were almost as difficult as my years of schooling had been. For much of that time I worked multiple jobs, and at one point I worked one full-time and three part-time jobs simultaneously. This included fixing vacuum cleaners for Bill Bush in the middle of the night. I still had a key to the store, and we communicated via scribbled notes left on the workbench. Often, we went for weeks at a time without seeing each other. But I was also doing after hours work for a couple of automotive shops, mostly suspension, carburetor, and automatic transmission work.

The Dart still served as my frequent daily transportation, but it sat parked whenever the weather forecast called for the chance of snow or ice, or whenever the salty aftermath of a winter storm remained on the roads. An accident in the summer of 1986 left the front end heavily damaged, but

I was able to repair it. Still, rust never sleeps, and I knew that the decay in the quarter panels, trunk extensions, outer wheel houses, and trunk floor was quietly spreading.

In the spring of 1987, I researched the parts I needed to retrofit disc brakes. I rounded up the necessary pieces, and I performed the conversion one night after work. I also rebuilt the front suspension again since most of it had to be changed anyway. As with the electronic ignition, kits for such retrofits are available today, but those kits didn't exist at that time. The Internet didn't exist either, so researching such projects was more difficult than it is today.

By the summer of 1987 I was working for a shop owned by two friends. Andy was clean-cut, good with people, and liked to play the part of the boss, yet he knew little about repairing cars. Fred was curmudgeonly and his mind housed an encyclopedia of dirty jokes, but he was highly intelligent and a gifted mechanic. He had a thirst for knowledge, and he was a whiz with electronics. Although they bickered like old women, they needed each other to survive in business. I had known both of them for a couple of years, but I had never met their families. That changed shortly after I began working for them when I met Kathy, Fred's daughter. She was nineteen and I was just shy of twenty-two. We enjoyed talking and laughing, so I asked her out to see a movie.

That movie was Fatal Attraction. At that time, I did not understand the mental instability of Glenn Close's character Alex Forrest, nor could I have known the prominent role that mental issues would play in our lives in the years to come.

After the movie, we weren't ready to call it an evening. Neither of us was hungry, and at nineteen she couldn't get into a bar, so we cruised around. It was a pleasant summer evening, so we headed to the winding roads of Beaver Valley. We talked and we laughed, enjoying each other's company. At the top of a long hill, I let off the accelerator and let the car coast. But as I pressed on the accelerator near the bottom of the hill, the car didn't respond. We coasted to a halt at the side of the dark, desolate road.

In the trunk I kept a twelve-volt trouble light that clipped onto the battery terminals, but nothing else. In the console was a screwdriver, but no other tools that would enable me to find and fix the problem. So, there I was, a mechanic, on a date with my boss's daughter, stuck on the side of the road with a broken-down car, and with no tools to fix it. What an embarrassing predicament! Of course, this was in the days before cell phones. I asked Kathy to crank the engine while I checked for spark. There was none. Oddly, the tachometer still registered engine speed. Suspecting a faulty ignition coil, I wiggled the terminals and wires. Miraculously, the car started! It ran poorly, and it cut off again a few miles later, but eventually I was able to limp it to Fred and Andy's shop where I had access to my tools and diagnostic equipment. That was also where my '66

Dodge truck was parked. Once there, I put the car inside the building, and we got into the truck.

The truck ran well, though it was an eyesore. Bits of dried glue that had once secured the long-absent headliner to the roof rained down on us at every bump. Even so, she laughed, so I laughed. The second half of the date didn't go at all as I had planned, but the night ended well. From that time on, we were nearly inseparable.

Late one afternoon in December I asked Fred if he would approve of me asking Kathy to marry me. He was ecstatic. Not long afterward, I proposed, and she accepted. We were married the following September. Although we got along well, we had a few disagreements, many of which came down to the Dart. She wanted me to sell it, and once I even tried to place it with a man who I thought would give it a good home. In retrospect, I am fortunate that he wasn't interested.

Two months before our wedding, we purchased a mobile home in a nice mobile home community near Smyrna, Delaware. We got it for a steal because the divorcee who owned it wanted to move back to her hometown of Blackwood, New Jersey in time to settle in before her son began kindergarten. Unlike most trailer parks, this one had off-street parking, and I was relieved knowing that the Dart would be safe in our own driveway. After we moved, my work commute was fifty miles each way. I drove the Dart occasionally in good weather, but I retired it from everyday use. Rarely did a day go by when I didn't see at least one accident during my travels, and I wasn't willing to risk damaging or destroying the car on a daily basis.

Two years later, we purchased a small ranch house five miles from the trailer park. We agreed that when we sold the trailer, we would use the proceeds to build a garage. I hired a crew to put in the foundation and to pour the floor, and then I built it from there. We had enough money to buy the materials, but not to pay for labor. It took eight months of evenings and weekends, and fortunately, I had help from my cousin David. The finished product was a three and a half car garage with ample attic space. I divided the two-bay storage side from the one and a half bay work side with a wall, and I insulated and drywalled the working area. I also wired the entire building for lights and outlets (on separate circuits for safety, so that if I tripped a breaker, I wouldn't be in sudden darkness) as well as air lines for compressed air. For the first time since its earliest years, the Dart now lived indoors.

The garage was barely finished when I dismantled the Dart. I repaired the body once more, installed new carpet and seat upholstery, repainted the dashboard and all of the interior trim, cleaned and repainted the engine, then painted the engine bay, trunk, door jambs, and the exterior of the car. I also installed a new vinyl top. Then I finished reassembling it in the spring of 1992. Although my body work skills were still far from professional, they had improved significantly over the previous nine years.

By then, I had been working for a Dodge dealership during the day for a couple of years, and I worked a variety of part-time jobs in the evening. Kathy hated that I was away so much, but with a new mortgage, the additional funds that we were applying to the principal every month, and her school expenses, I had no choice but to work long hours. When I was at home, I immersed myself in projects because there were many things in and around the house that needed attention. Furthermore, I feared that if I didn't, laziness would overcome me. As a task-oriented person, being able to cross items off my to-do list afforded me great satisfaction.

For as long as I had known Kathy, she had been a part-time college student working toward a degree in elementary education. She worked full-time as a pre-school teacher, primarily with four-year-olds, and she had also been the director of one pre-school. After moving into the house, she attended college full-time and worked part-time. She graduated Magna cum Laude in the spring of 1993.

The excitement of graduating faded quickly, however, when it proved difficult for her to find a full-time teaching position. Some of her school friends accepted long-term substitute positions in hopes that they would lead to full-time positions, but Kathy would not. As she saw it, she had paid her dues. But soon, a darkness settled over her and her behavior changed. She was moody and sullen most of the time. She came to care little about the things that used to be important to her, and she was quick to snap at me. She also developed an unnatural animosity toward the Dart. She said things like, "If anything happens to you, I'm giving you a burial at sea in that damned car." I brushed off those comments, but her mental state worsened as the weeks and months ticked by. She was unable to work, and soon she was seeing a counselor. Often she made remarks to the effect that life wasn't worth the effort. During the short days of winter, I'd drive home from work to find her car in the driveway, but our house dark. Fearing the worst, I would make my way inside. Often, I would find her sitting in the living room, expressionless, and staring into the darkness.

Early in the spring of 1994, she had a meltdown and spent several days in a mental hospital. When she returned home, she was quite different—positive, and determined to rebuild her life and move forward. Unfortunately, this new-found positivity didn't last. Thus began the cycle of frequent hospital stays followed by extreme highs, and then extreme lows. Her deteriorating condition soon led to a series of suicide attempts.

During this time, in addition to pleading with doctors, hospitals, and the insurance company to obtain the best possible care for her, I navigated a financial minefield as I tried to keep everyone paid. We were living on my income alone, and as a flat-rate auto mechanic I had to be on my game to keep my productivity high, for my pay was based solely on how much work I produced. Many times, I sought solace behind the wheel of the Dart while I saw cracks spreading through the foundation of our world. It was only a matter of time before it would all come crashing down. How could I keep her safe while still holding down a fulltime job? What more could I do to help her?

I often thought about a conversation I'd had with my grandfather when I was about ten. We were on a supply run, driving in his '69 International pick-up truck somewhere on U.S. Route 50 near Salisbury. He told the story about my biological grandmother's death, which had occurred in 1955 as a result of a car accident when the family was on its first and only vacation. My father was thirteen at the time, and he had nearly lost his life as well. Later, his injuries caused him to be rejected by every branch of the military, and they also prompted him to seek a career without the physical demands of carpentry. My father had told me the story a number of times, but hearing it from my grandfather, I gained a different perspective. As he talked, I got a sense of how his life and his family had been shattered. His injuries were minor by comparison to my father's and grandmother's, but in the days following the accident he had become a single father of four. He had remarried just a few months later, as much out of necessity as love.

It had been twenty years since he had been widowed, but from the desperation in his voice and the expression on his face, I could see that he was reliving the emotions as if they were fresh. He had interred them in a shallow grave in the back of his mind two decades prior, but such emotions seldom stay buried. Although I was too young to appreciate all that he had been through, I understood that it had been traumatic for him. I also came away with a strong feeling that his experience might somehow foreshadow a similar crisis in my own life. Would I, too, be widowed? I now knew the answer to that question: in a sense, yes.

Watching someone who I loved drown in the abyss of mental illness was the hardest thing I have ever had to do. I was powerless to intervene or to alter her course. All I could do was watch helplessly as she spiraled downward. When a person dies from a physical cause, loved ones might question the reason for the death, but they do not question what caused it. The cause is easy to understand—illness or injury has interrupted the body's life functions. But when a person "dies" in the figurative sense due to mental illness, there is no physical death. The cause of the "death" cannot be understood; consequently, loved ones grapple with it in vain. There is no coming to terms with it. In short, there is no closure.

By the spring of 1995, it had become clear that the hospitals in Delaware could not help her. We were referred to a hospital northwest of Philadelphia. With our annual insurance allowance for mental health already depleted, this institution wanted several thousand dollars up front before they would admit her. I sold two of our cars, and once again the

Dart was on the chopping block. Again, it didn't sell. Kathy went away for what was supposed to be a two week stay. She did not come home for two months. When she did, she had been through such a transformation that I didn't know who she was. She looked the same, but she was a different person. I wasn't sure if it was due to the treatment she had received or the cocktail of medications she was on, but this Kathy was a stranger. She started doing things that were unpredictable and not at all like her old self. First, she moved one of her hospital mates into our house under the premise that being together would help to make them both strong. But when she found that her friend had hidden a bottle of liquor under the lid of our cats' litter box, she threw her friend out. Then, on the weekend of my thirtieth birthday, she went to another friend's house somewhere in Philadelphia for a few days. I spent that rainy weekend alone, working on the Dart, and listening to the new Wanderlust album while consumed with worry over my wife, our finances, and our future.

When the bill from the hospital arrived in the mail, it was nearly 50,000 dollars in addition to what we had already paid. They made an "administrative adjustment" which brought the price of her transformation down by about twenty percent, but the writing was on the wall. We were financially sunk. Everything we had worked for was nullified by this debt.

One evening shortly after we received this bill, she had an epiphany. She said, "Every time I fall apart, you are there to pick up the pieces. You make sure I get the help I need."

I nodded and said, "Yeah, that's my job. For better or worse, remember?"

She continued, "But as long as I have you, I'm never going to have to stand on my own. That means I'm never going to get any better." Then she said she wanted to separate.

I was stunned. Was this a trick of the meds? Did she really believe this? Then she said she wanted us to start dating all over again, and to also date other people. Had her therapist planted this seed in her mind and then nourished it? I didn't know, but it didn't matter.

What I did know was that if we weren't going to be together, I couldn't ride this roller coaster any longer. I could not continue to care for her if we were not husband and wife. We talked over the next week or so, and then I told her she had to make a decision: either we were married or we weren't. There was no in-between. She moved out on Labor Day weekend.

Oddly, we remained friendly through our separation and subsequent divorce. Seated across from each other at a table in the library near the courthouse in Wilmington, we listed our assets and our liabilities, and we divided them as evenly as we could before filing the paperwork. On the day of our divorce hearing, she picked me up at work and we drove to the courthouse together. Afterward, with our divorce finalized, we hurried across town so that we could complete the paperwork enabling me to refinance the house in my name only. She had agreed to take the contents of the house as well as the building lot we had purchased outright a few years earlier. I had agreed to keep the house and my tools, and we had split the hospital debt down the middle.

As I had done during other troubling times in my life, I sought peace behind the wheel of the Dart often. Through the years, much of my best thinking had taken place there, and my post-marriage era was no different. Although I had not always been the perfect husband, I had done my best, and I had been faithful, caring, and devoted. Consequently, I carried little guilt as I set out to rediscover and redefine myself not as half of a couple, but as an individual. Frequent cruises in the Dart helped to soothe my troubled mind. Although I was far from whole, driving that car made me feel as whole as I could be. The car and I had been through so much together already, and I knew we would get through this too. Meanwhile, I threw myself into work and school. In addition, for a few years I had been writing technical how-to articles for a handful of national magazines. Soon, I ramped up my freelance writing too. Because each story I wrote required a series of photographs that complemented the text, the Dart figured prominently into my freelance work.

By 1997, I was working full-time, earning a degree in Automotive Technology as a full-time student, and writing regularly. I was also involved in the first real relationship since my divorce, although it ended that spring.

Steve and I had casually talked about competing in what was then known as the Cannonball One Lap of America. The "One Lap" event occurred annually, and it was an outgrowth of the Cannonball Baker Sea to Shining Sea Memorial Trophy Dash, more commonly known as the Cannonball Run. While the original Cannonball event had been a clandestine and illegal race from New York City to Redondo Beach, California, the One Lap events involved driving around the country while making time trials at various racetracks over the course of a week. Rick Ehrenberg, the technical editor of Mopar Action magazine, was a regular competitor in One Lap, and both Steve and I were quite familiar with his annual write-ups of the competition. Competing in One Lap had been a dream for each of us, but it was Steve who insisted that we could actually do it. In the spring of 1997, we acquired a 1970 Dodge Dart from our mutual friend, Rob McCall. Working diligently over the next year, we transformed it from a junkyard refugee into a serious competitor on the various road courses we would encounter. In the midst of all of this, early that summer I signed the contract with CarTech Publishing, Incorporated to write my first book, Chrysler Performance Upgrades.

In the fall of 1997, I was extremely busy, but things were moving on course. The One Lap Dart as it was now known, was progressing well and I had made significant progress on the book. One topic that I covered in the book was how to build a big block V-8 powered A-body (Dart, Valiant, and the other compacts based on Chrysler's small rear wheel drive platform). For this, I built another '68 Dart, this one powered by a 383 cubic inch V-8. Of course, I also covered various aspects of the build of the One Lap Dart in the book, and I was involved in a few other projects that other friends had going on. Consequently, I had access to all of the photographic material that I needed.

It was also in the fall when Debbie, a close friend from high school, was married. By now, I had become friends with her husband too. At their wedding reception, I was introduced to a sweet and funny woman named Kristan. We dated for a couple of months, and I really liked this girl! The problem was that although she was separated, she was not yet divorced. Soon I saw that her narcissistic and manipulative estranged husband still held power over her and their children. Consequently, we agreed to break things off. Of course, the Dart was my greatest coping mechanism during that time. Soon, I began dating another woman, Anna, but things just weren't the same. She was no Kristan.

I graduated college in December 1997, and I finished the book in the spring of 1998. In May, Steve and I competed in that year's One Lap of America where we won third place in the Vintage American class. As summer came around, I finally had time to devote to some of my own projects and to rest. In retrospect I knew that neither the book nor One Lap would have happened if not for my '68 Dart. Many of the topics I had written about and many of the modifications we had made to the One Lap Dart had been developed on my '68 Dart over the preceding years.

In August, Anna and I attended the Mopar Nationals, a three-day car show, swap meet, and drag racing event held annually in Columbus, Ohio. I hadn't been to the Nationals in many years, and she had never been, but it was her idea to go. To this day I cannot fathom why she wanted to go, for she had no interest in cars. Of course, we drove my Dart, but it turned out that a long road trip in a car with loud exhaust and no air conditioning wasn't as fun as she had thought it would be, and she made sure I knew it. Progress was slower than we would have liked, due in part to heavy traffic, but mostly because of a turn that I missed. It was mid-afternoon when we reached the I-70 and I-76 split on the Pennsylvania Turnpike.

As I slowed for the ramp to exit the turnpike, I pressed the clutch pedal and attempted to downshift from fourth gear to third, but the shifter wouldn't budge! Soon we were sitting on the shoulder with the transmission locked in fourth gear, facing uphill, and unable to move. Anna mumbled not quite under her breath while I yanked and shoved the shifter frantically. Sweat dripped from my face and arms. I cursed our misfortune while she cursed my car. Suddenly I thought back to that fateful night with Kathy more than a decade earlier. Had my Dart been trying to warn me then? And was it repeating that warning now? Was God speaking to me through the car? Under my breath I said, "I hear what you are telling me." Immediately, the shifter popped out of gear as if nothing was wrong! We continued on our way with no further trouble. That transmission remained in the car, untouched, for nearly fifteen years afterward.

When we arrived in Columbus, we checked into the motel and then headed to Brice Road. While daytime activities took place at the nearby National Trail Raceway, in the evening, folks headed to Brice Road for cruising. There, cars crept from one end of the road to the other while spectators flanked both sides. Police officers stood at regular intervals along the double yellow lines at the center of the road monitoring the action. They permitted cruisers to do small burnouts provided they kept their cars going straight and didn't get out of hand. Anna didn't derive any fun from cruising, and one of the times when traffic came to a stop she stated, "I think burnouts are stupid!" Just then, there was a splash in the road directly in front of us. A kid standing on the sidewalk was holding an empty bucket while looking at us. He yelled, "Come on, light 'em up! Impress the lady!" He was pumping his arm, nearly overcome with enthusiasm.

Not being one to disappoint a kid, I rolled into the water, brought the RPMs up, dumped the clutch, and matted the accelerator. I went through first gear and into second before the tail of the Dart began to swing to the right, though we hadn't moved more than a few feet forward. Immediately, I let off the gas and pressed in the clutch, and we crept away under the watchful eye of a police officer. Anna sat smug, certain that I was about to receive a ticket, but the cop waved us on instead. The rest of the trip was uneventful save for our quarrelling. We broke up shortly afterward.

Within a week of our breakup, Kristan called. We hadn't spoken in months, but she was now divorced and ready to move on. This was in the fall of 1998. We resumed dating, and our relationship flourished. In November, the Delaware Valley Mopar Association hosted a Saturday evening gathering at a restaurant in southeastern Pennsylvania about ninety minutes away. Kristan knew the history of the Dart, and we were both nervous as we set out for the trip. To our delight, the car gave no hint of trouble. In fact, I would swear it ran better than usual.

On a warm, sunny day the following April, Kristan, her mother, her daughter Erin, and I all piled into the Dart and drove to a Justice of the Peace court where Kristan and I exchanged vows. Two weeks later, Kristan and I drove the Dart to our first of many Northeast Hemi Owners Association car club meets. In the more than two decades since then, we have driven it to meets in Pennsylvania, New York, our home state Delaware, and all-over New England, including Cape Cod. It has also made a couple of 1400 mile round trips to the north woods of Maine. In 2004, Erin, Kristan and I took fast laps around Watkins Glen International Raceway. This was especially fun, for I had competed at The Glen in two races a week apart during One Lap of America in 1998, and I was glad for them to finally experience one of the tracks they had heard me mention numerous times.

Regarding my father, our strained relationship continued for a number of years. In July, 1992 he was downsized from his job mere months before he was eligible for his pension. It was a severe blow to him, and the family gathered at my parents' house that evening. Still reeling from his gut-punch earlier that day, he seemed bewildered and lost. It occurred to me that, unlike me, he had never had to change jobs. He had begun working for Hercules, Inc. while he was in college, and he had continued working for Hercules until that day 29 years later. But although the thought of finding another job seemed daunting, I knew my father, and I knew his will and determination. I told him, "However this turns out, you will land on your feet. You're going to be okay." It was a coincidence that I had driven the Dart to work that day, but I was glad that I had. As I started the engine before heading home, Boston's Peace of Mind began playing on the radio. Was my car giving me a message? Was God reassuring me? Was He was speaking to me through the car? And had He actually been doing so all along? I didn't know, but I found this thought comforting. No matter where the message came from, it wasn't lost on me.

And Dad was fine. A few months later, he converted the garage into an office where he ran his accounting business for the next 25 years. I stopped by one weekend during construction to help with the drywall. I had driven the Dart that day, and when he and I had to run out to pick up some small supplies we took my car. As we motored through the neighborhood where I had grown up, Dad thanked me for believing in him at a time when he couldn't believe in himself. After a period of floundering, he finally felt that he was moving forward, just as I was sure that he would. We talked briefly, then the conversation fell quiet. At once he said, "You know, the problems you had with me were the same problems I had with my father. The difference is that you had the balls enough to do something about it." I was stunned. I don't remember what I said, or if I said anything at all.

My grandfather had grown up poor, but he had found prosperity as a self-employed carpenter. He was proud to have earned enough money to raise a family and to live comfortably. My father had grown up in a blue-collar family, and he was proud to have been the first in his family to go to college, earn multiple degrees, and embark on a career in corporate America. He had been appalled by my desire to go backwards! Though I believe his actions were misguided, I now understood that he had been trying to save me from myself. Regardless of whether he had been right or wrong to do so, I felt that he and I reached a new plateau that day.

In 2005, Dad suffered his first stroke. I was at work when I got the call, and immediately I headed to the hospital. Once again, when I got into the car, Boston's <u>Peace of Mind</u> was playing on the radio. I smiled, for I was sure that he would be okay. I believe that God was speaking to me through the car once again. Dad survived this stroke and two more, and he lived for another seventeen years.

I had driven the Dart to automotive school on my first day, and I drove it on the day that I graduated. I drove it to work on my first day as an auto mechanic, and I drove it to work on my last day as a full-time mechanic. I drove it to work on my first day as a full-time teacher when I took over a high school automotive program in 2006, and I plan to drive it to work on the day when I retire from teaching. Kristy and I drove it to my second college graduation in 2016. I drove it to my hypnotherapist's appointment on the day that I quit smoking, and I spent New Year's Eve in 2018 cleaning it while consuming alcohol for the last time. In addition, our middle grandson Riley and I drove it to numerous car shows and cruises when he was a pre-teen, and I really miss those days. The Dart played a critical role in launching me into each of my three careers: automotive technician, automotive journalist, and automotive teacher. In 2016, the Slant Six that I had built in 1984 gave way to a 340 cubic inch V-8, but the car's spirit remains as strong as ever.

I didn't set out to keep the Dart for 40 years, and I really didn't believe the rusty body would last that long, but I didn't begin this journey with plans to let it go either. I am thankful that I was unsuccessful both times I tried to place it with a new owner. Was it divine intervention? I like to think so. At this point, I intend to keep it for the rest of my days. I still plan to restore the body properly, and I have all of the replacement body panels to do so, but I will probably have to wait until I'm retired. I don't want to leave it disassembled for as long as it will take to restore while I'm still working full-time because I'm having too much fun driving it!

I have to wonder, how would my life have turned out if not for this car? How would I be earning a living? Would I be married? If so, to whom? Would I have a family as wonderful as the one I that Kristan and her children welcomed me into? Above all, would I be happy? I cannot answer these questions, but I also cannot imagine being happier or more fulfilled than I am. Life has never been easy, but I have enjoyed a constant, though inanimate, companion. I have had many experiences, learned many lessons, and made countless friends through my car connections. Few of these blessings would have come my way if not for my Dart.

One Woman's Two Greatest Loves

While some folks rotate through cars regularly, most of us keep our cars for years or even decades. A few of us, however, are lucky enough to have had our cars since our formative years. Jenni Romano is one such woman, for she has owned her '73 Charger SE for 25 years—more than half of her life. Although we all experience ups and downs, some experience more than their share of hardships. Jenni is one such person. Her friendly demeanor belies the physical and emotional pain she has endured. Her multiple disabilities relegate her to walking with a cane, but they don't stop her from working on or driving her car—often exuberantly!

Jenni's Charger was a gift from an ex-boyfriend. She describes her first impression of it as, "Poetry in motion. My ex-boyfriend told me, 'When you sit in this car, there's a fire in your eyes that I have never seen before.'" She named her car Holley. "She's green, has a Holley carburetor, and I got her for Christmas."

The 22-year-old Jenni was no stranger to fast cars. By then she had already owned a few, and she was a regular in the local street racing scene in New Jersey. The Charger, however, was more potent than any of her other cars had been. "My ex took out the eight-track and the air conditioning. He also took out the original 400 cubic inch engine. It's okay, though. I love my 440! I was told it came out of a '67 GTX, but the (identification) stamping is hard to read."

In the years that followed, Jenni enjoyed her Charger, and she raced it often on the street and at both Englishtown and Atco dragstrips. Although equipped with a highway friendly axle ratio and open differential, the heavy Charger regularly earned thirteen-second time slips. "The rear is set up for highway vs. speed. I squealed halfway down the damn track!"

Although memories such as these form strong bonds between owners and cars, for some the bonds grow much stronger. Jenni describes her relationship as, "A love story. She saved me and gave me a place to belong right when I needed her the most. All of the traumas I have experienced dissolve when I'm in the driver's seat."

As a female who was drawn to the male-dominated world of automobiles, her main inspiration came from the movie Better Off Dead. "When I was 11 years old, I saw that little French girl fix the Camaro, and I knew right then that's who I wanted to be." She was further inspired by Marisa Tomei's character, Mona Lisa Vito, in the movie My Cousin Vinny. Jenni learned much of what she knows about working on cars from friends, but she is mostly self-taught. In addition to keeping her Charger running for more than two decades, she also works on her everyday car, a high mileage Chevy HHR. "I've been called a motor head or gear head. No gender identity in those names. But I've gotten marriage proposals from guys who called me a car chick." She prefers older cars to newer ones. "When this world goes all Mad Max Thunderdome, you ain't gonna see any Prius on the road!"

About that special bond she enjoys with her Charger, she said, "As car enthusiasts, everyone has a reason for why their car is so precious to them. On (Monday) December 13, 2010, I lost a seventeen-year battle with infertility. I went under the knife for the sixth and final time for an emergency hysterectomy. The five previous surgeries were all to remove recurring multiple tumors as a double dose of a bad gene from both parents, but the last time, the fight was over. In that last surgery, I was completely removed from society as a woman. (I was) completely forced out like being ostracized from the biggest club in the human race. From that day on, I have had no common ground with women at social or family events. I cannot share stories of childbirth, diapers, teething, PTA meetings, fevers, homework, and everything that women share with each other. (I do not belong to) the club where men and women fall in love and start families, then move to the next chapter in life. In the 25 years that I have owned my Charger, I have had wonderful adventures and memories, but I also found a 'club' that I belonged in. In my car is the only place where I don't feel like an awkward misfit. So, it's not just the fact that she's the only thing that never let me down. I've lost a lot of meaningful things in my life, including my ability to give life. My Charger is the one thing that no one has ever been able to take away from me. She makes me feel like I belong—accepted and normal. She's more than just a car. She's my solace. She saved me, and I call her my home. My demons can't catch me in this car."

Of course, owning her car has brought her into contact with many good people, and it has fostered a number of friendships. "Car enthusiasts are special people. The Mopar community is especially tight knit. It's a real family atmosphere." Her Charger has also brought about experiences that she wouldn't have had otherwise. On Wednesday, May 2, 2018 she and her Charger appeared on the Discovery Channel's show Sticker Shock. "They transported my car to South Gate, California near Los Angeles. It was filmed in an abandoned Firestone tire warehouse." The whole experience came about because Jenni answered a casting call. "The criteria was a lot of history and great stories. I filled out the application during a blizzard, and less than four hours later, Beverly Hills, California came up (on Caller ID) as an incoming call. Sure enough, it was the Discovery Channel. They called me the quintessential Jersey girl!"

Although her Charger means everything to her, Jenni's situation necessitates that the car remains outdoors. "I have no garage, so every tool imaginable is in that trunk—jack stands, wheel chocks, floor jack, torque wrench, three or four toolboxes, oil, trans fluid, spare hoses, spare parts, possibly a body—just kidding!"

In 2018, Jenni walked away from her abusive marriage. She worked, saved, and purchased a home a year later. Since then, "Holley" has received some much-needed attention. Her flanks have been smoothed and a new coat of green paint now accentuates her gentle curves.

In addition, a new man has entered Jenni's life, thanks in no small part to Holley. The couple met at a local cruise event, and their instant friendship eventually blossomed into much more. His name is Rich, and he is a car enthusiast as well. He has owned his '70 Road Runner convertible for more than forty years. The two were engaged in the presence of dozens of friends at the All Chrysler Nationals in Carlisle, Pennsylvania in July, 2020. She said, "We met because of our cars, and then we fell in love. Our dedication to our cars has grown into a dedication to each other in a wonderful, loving relationship."

Through the years, the spirit of Jenni's Charger has remained very much alive, strong and feisty. It not only mirrors its owner, it is an extension of her. And now, it has a Road Runner cruise mate.

Retrieving a Georgia Lemon

My buddy Steve and I met more than forty years ago when I was a shy sixteen-year-old working at a vacuum cleaner and sewing machine repair shop near Wilmington, Delaware. As introverted as I was, Steve was every bit as extroverted. While I was content to sit at my bench repairing broken machines, he was in his element on the sales floor helping customers. Despite our very different personalities we became friends, and one thing we shared was a passion for cars. Steve's first car had been a lime green '70 Dart Swinger, and for years he'd longed for another. By 1996 he owned the store, now called Steve's Sew-'n'-Vac, and the hunt was on for a car similar to his first.

One of Steve's most admirable qualities is his ability to look and to think beyond the invisible barriers that most folks place before themselves. He embraces the mantra, "If you don't ask, the answer will always be no." While ordinary folks might dismiss an idea as "can't be done," Steve's approach is to say, "I know there's a way, and I'm going to find it."

One day in early 1996 he proposed a trip to Georgia to visit his mother and to pick up a preserved 1970 Dodge Dart Swinger 340—a lime green beauty much like his first car. Steve's mother Jane, long widowed, had relocated from Delaware to Georgia more than a decade earlier. Her significant other, Russ, seemed to have his fingers in everything automotive. He owned a repair shop with a used car lot and a small junkyard, he built dirt track racing engines for local racers, and he fielded dirt track racecars of his own from time to time over the years. His connections had led him to the Dart, and he had purchased it for Steve. "Russ said it's in pretty good shape. He checked the car over and fixed a few minor things," Steve said. "Right now, he's working on the heater." Heat was a must in February.

I was the shop foreman in a Chrysler-Jeep dealership by day and a college student by night. I'm a sucker for adventure, but I couldn't be away from work and school for an extended time. I told Steve that I had no choice but to decline, and I thought that was the end of the discussion.

Steve didn't see it that way. "I got a deal on plane tickets," he said over the phone a few days later. He was talking fast so I couldn't interrupt. "We'll fly out of Baltimore Sunday morning, land in Charlotte, and then catch a connecting flight to Spartanburg. My mom will pick us up there, take us to her house, and we'll be on the road by noon. It's a twelve-hour drive so we'll be back by midnight." He paused to let it sink in, but only for a moment. Knowing I'd object, he rattled on, "And if things go wrong, I got round trip tickets. The return trip is scheduled for Tuesday, but we can change our departure time for the return trip for fifty bucks a ticket and fly home that night." Damn it, he knew how to defuse any argument I could muster! This was not my first time thinking that he might be crazy— far from it, actually. But the opportunity for adventure was so far off the scale that I just couldn't say no.

Our bumpy red-eye from Baltimore to Charlotte was via a DC-9— essentially a school bus with wings. We were to depart Charlotte an hour later, but as we walked into the airport I spotted an overhead monitor which showed that our connecting flight had been cancelled. I swatted Steve's arm and pointed at the monitor. "Oh no! That won't do!" he exclaimed. He stormed up to the information desk ahead.

"We booked you on a later flight," the desk attendant stated as if she had personally done us a favor. Steve voiced his displeasure, but the attendant sat stone-faced, unfazed. It seemed her job was to take grief from angry travelers, and she was good at it.

We should have landed ninety miles away in Spartanburg an hour and a half later. We realized that we could rent a car and drive that distance, arriving on schedule. Minutes later, we were thumping down the interstate at breakneck speed in a ragged Chevy Cavalier rental car with one misshapen tire.

The Greenville-Spartanburg airport was an unimposing facility half the size of a rural high school. We scanned the parking lot but failed to locate Jane's car. We dashed up and down every corridor, and we searched the waiting areas and the café, but there was no sign of her. In this pre-cell phone era, we could only assume she'd left upon learning we'd been moved to a later flight. Three hours later she appeared with Russ in tow, moments before our rescheduled flight landed. "We saw your flight was canceled, so we went shopping," Jane said. Russ looked exhausted. It was now after noon.

We piled into Jane's Dodge Raider. As we drove, Russ disclosed the specifics of the Dart, and the more he said, the more uneasy I became. "It was sitting 'bout ten years. The boy pushed it into the woods when he parked it, but we drug it out and got it running." WHAT??? I thought. What does the brake system look like? How much rust and crap is in the gas tank? Russ continued, "It runs real good, but it don't always shift into high gear." Oh swell! Twelve hours of interstate driving ahead of us, and what's the one gear we need the most? "If I didn't mention it, it's got a little sore spot on the left side near the back. And I didn't get the heater finished, but it's in the trunk." With the heater missing, I knew there was an open stovepipe-sized hole in the firewall that would channel cold air and engine fumes directly into the passenger's crotch. "It's been warm so you shouldn't need heat." Indeed, northern Georgians were enjoying unseasonably warm sixty-degree highs, but in Delaware the highs were in the twenties and the ground was covered in snow. I wanted to punch Steve.

When we pulled up at Jane's place the excitement on Steve's face faded to horror. There sat his Dart on decayed tires, its sagging rear springs lending a nose-up attitude, its body and windows chalked green with woods funk. And that "little sore spot" turned out to be a foot-deep crater where the quarter panel appeared to have been clobbered by a dump truck. The collision had folded the rear bumper, leaving it jutting from the back of the car for more than a foot.

We scrubbed the windows and headed to a nearby gas station where we filled the tank. Then we sought the interstate and pointed the front-end north as the sun hung low in the western sky. The worn suspension made it difficult to stay it in one lane. Every expansion joint caused us to change direction, but it was impossible to predict which way the car would veer. A makeshift roadside alignment did little to improve the handling. Even so, it ran surprisingly well—right up to the moment that it quit. Five miles into our journey, the engine began to sputter and lose power as if it were running out of fuel. We coasted to the side of the road. I was nearly certain that the fuel filter was clogged, but when I went to remove it I discovered that there was no fuel filter. Someone had plumbed a rubber hose between the fuel pump and the carburetor, thus eliminating the filter. That meant that sediment from the rusted gas tank had clogged the fuel pick-up sock inside the tank. We knew we couldn't remove it while the tank was full, so the only thing we could do was to blow backward through the fuel line and into the tank in hopes of freeing some of the debris from the sock. After a mouthful of rotten gasoline, I was able to blow into the fuel line. I reconnected it, and we were on our way once more. Unfortunately, I had to repeat this process a mile later, and then a mile after that, and again after another mile. We were losing hope and the sun was sinking fast.

While we pondered our plight a roll-back pulled up behind us. "You boys need help?" the driver called to us. Steve spoke to him, flashed a credit card, and in short order the operator loaded the ailing Dart and took us back to the airport. There we would implement Steve's contingency plan to fly home. As we bounced down the interstate in the rollback, Steve said he would talk to Russ and arrange to have the Dart transported later.

It was after dark when we unloaded the car in the airport parking lot. The ratty, beat-up, moss-covered car might have looked at home in Russ's junkyard, but it couldn't have looked more out of place among the shiny newer cars that now surrounded it. Under different circumstances we would have found this funny, but we had no time for humor. We ran inside to catch a plane.

The desk attendant informed us that the tickets for the return flight wouldn't become valid until Tuesday. The fifty-dollar deal to reschedule our return flights would apply only if we re-booked our return flights for some time after Tuesday. If we wanted to fly home that night the cost would be over six hundred dollars each. Steve ranted again, but she remained as cool, emotionless, and unbending as the attendant we'd encountered in Charlotte. It was as if they were sisters.

Soon we were bound for home in another rented car, thankfully this time with four round tires. We alternated driving and sleeping, but somewhere near Richmond I confused the two. I awoke to Steve's shouts only to realize that I was driving.

As the sun of a new day overtook the darkness, I collapsed onto his couch. I blinked, and then I got up and headed to work.

It was our best trip ever!

Rusty's Reprieve

Unlike most educators, teaching has been a second career for me. I'm a lifelong car nut, and from my earliest days it was only natural that my first career choice would be guided by my lust for automobiles and all things mechanical. I've been an ASE certified Master Automobile Technician since I was twenty and I spent the next two decades working fulltime in various shops and dealerships as a line technician and shop foreman. In retrospect, the most meaningful period of my time in the automotive business was when I worked as the foreman of the shop in a small Chrysler-Jeep dealership in Elkton, Maryland. Barely thirty, I was the go-to guy for half a dozen ambitious, yet largely untrained, budding technicians who were in their early twenties. That, and my later experience as the stepfather of a couple of great kids whom I love dearly, served as the catalyst for my new career in education.

I began teaching evening classes in Automotive Technology at Delaware Technical and Community College in January 2003. In the fall of 2006 I left the field when I accepted a fulltime position teaching Automotive Technology at Caroline Career and Technology Center, a small trade and technical high school on Maryland's sleepy Eastern Shore. I knew that teaching kids would be much different from working with adults, but it took me a couple of years to really learn how to relate to the kids. Unlike adults, I had to entice them to learn, and I had to do so on their level.

My wife Kristy and I have several old cars, and on occasion I'd bring one of them to school for the kids to see. I also do some work for other classic car owners in the area, and I've invited many of them to visit the school and speak to the students. No matter what project I'm involved in, I try to share as much of it with the class as possible in an effort to help them realize that there's more to an auto technician's life than repairing broken down mini-vans and soccer mom SUVs. As I see it, the automotive realm is more a lifestyle than it is an occupation. Either you live a life of cars or you don't.

In August, 2008 I spotted an ad for a tattered 1964 Dodge Dart. It had a 170 cubic inch Slant Six and a column-shifted three-speed manual transmission. It didn't run, there were no seats, most of the floor was gone, and it was missing several pieces. What wasn't missing was rusted, and judging by the condition of the floor, I was sure the frame rails had been attacked by the tin worms as well. I deemed it too far gone to save, but Kristy and I already owned two other '64 Darts and I was sure this one still held some parts that we could use. The auction opened at 150 dollars, and a bid in that amount had already been placed. It was nearby and reasonably priced, and when the auction ended it was ours.

I towed it to school, and the next day we tossed in a battery and connected a gas can to the engine. It fired right up and ran remarkably well. Upon closer inspection we discovered that despite its shabby appearance and rust-eaten floor, the frame rails were solid and the car was structurally sound. Even so, I insisted that this car was to be a parts donor. I didn't want or need another project. But soon I was reminded that sometimes projects take on a life of their own despite our initial convictions to the contrary.

For more than a year the car remained in running, yet dilapidated condition. Owing to its simple and uncluttered design I found it perfect for teaching charging system and starting system diagnosis, compression and cylinder leakage tests, and torsion bar suspensions. The left rear brake hemorrhaged fluid, so two students swapped in a used wheel cylinder from another Dart we'd dismantled a year earlier. Of course, in order to drive the car into and out of the shop I needed a place to sit. My makeshift seat consisted of an old wheel and tire, strategically placed so as to not fall through the holes in the floor, and covered with upholstery fashioned from a piece of corrugated cardboard. Eventually we began referring to the car as Rusty.

During a class discussion in the fall of 2009 a group of students confronted me concerning Rusty's future. To my surprise, they had grown fond of the old junker, and they didn't want me to break it up for parts even though I'd stated all along that was the plan. They were all regular viewers of the TV shows Pinks and Pass Time, and they urged me to build Rusty into a drag racer instead.

At first I resisted. The school could not own or sponsor a racecar, so all of the expenses for such a project would be mine to bear.

Furthermore, many of the required modifications fell outside of the curriculum, so I couldn't devote class time to teaching them. I would have to do all of that work myself on my own time. With limited resources, any time or money I spent building a racecar would delay my progress on the other projects Kristy and I had. But I also knew that such a project would spark the kids' interest, and I could easily address many of the topics we cover in our program while building the car. Moreover, I knew that once the word got out, an on-going project such as this could attract future students, and it might even help boost parent and community awareness and involvement in our program.

Then I considered my personal cache of spare parts. I already had all of the major driveline components we would need. They included a low mileage rebuilt 318 cubic inch V-8, a rebuildable A-904 automatic transmission, and an 8.25-inch rear axle along with a 4.10:1 ratio ring and pinion and a limited slip differential. I also had a pair of fenderwell headers that had been given to me years earlier by one of my students at Delaware Tech. Furthermore, I had access to some of the necessary race-oriented parts through my connections with friends. I mentioned my thoughts to Kristy. She wasn't thrilled for the progress of our 1970 Dodge Challenger to be delayed, but she supported this new project. Yes, it was feasible to build a super low buck drag racer from this rotting hulk of a Dart!

Before doing any major mechanical work we had to repair the floor. For this I enlisted the help of the Industrial Technology class because their program includes metal fabrication and welding. I drove the car into their shop, and within two days a couple of overly zealous students had chopped out all of the rusted floor sections as well as the parking brake cables, brake line, and the trunk transition behind the rear seat, which was not rusted. Ugh! Meanwhile, the student who had been chosen by the teacher to do the welding had landed himself in some serious trouble and would not return to the program. At that time, he had no other students capable of making the necessary floor repairs.

I knew little about welding, but I realized that if this project was to progress any further I would have to learn. I'm still not a good welder, but under the tutelage of the Industrial Tech teacher I fabricated and installed frame connectors and built a new floor one small section at a time.

By the end of the school year, I had also built the rear axle and scored a pair of used Super Stock drag race leaf springs. My students rebuilt the front and rear suspension, installed the new axle, and rebuilt the brake system utilizing a dual master cylinder in place of the early single master cylinder for safety. We didn't work on the car every day, but they remained excited about it and they soon learned that being allowed to work on it was a privilege that they could earn by doing well on their required work.

When school got underway the following year we addressed the V-8 engine that we would use. I had a pair of cylinder heads from a 360 reconditioned by a local machine shop. The 360 heads have larger valves and ports than the 318 heads, and they are a worthwhile upgrade on a performance-built 318. After I received them back from the machine shop, a couple of students disassembled them for porting. This is a tricky and time-consuming procedure, and one slip of the hand-held cutter can destroy a head. I explained what porting was all about and why we were doing it. We also had several lengthy discussions about valve timing and camshaft degreeing as the engine went back together. While these are generally race-only practices, a basic understanding of these topics helps students to understand what the engineers who design cars must consider and why they make many of the choices they do. It also provides a foundation of knowledge that makes the theory behind today's engines with variable valve timing easier to grasp.

In the meantime, I rebuilt and modified an automatic transmission, and I installed a shift kit that provides full manual control of the valve body. I also scoured junkyards, swap meets, and eBay, eventually amassing a pile of used parts including an Edelbrock Torker intake manifold, an Edelbrock 750 CFM four-barrel carburetor, a racing ratchet shifter, a lightweight racing seat, a five-gallon fuel cell, a trunk-mounted battery box, a pair of repairable fenders, and a driver's door. A good friend and benefactor of our program donated some miscellaneous mechanical pieces including a Comp Magnum 280H camshaft package and a torque converter, while another longtime friend came through with a pair of vintage Cragar S/S five-spoke chrome wheels for the front. A student offered a matching pair of Cragars for the rear at a very reasonable price.

In early December the students removed the six-cylinder engine and three-speed manual transmission along with the front-end body panels. During winter break I test-fitted the new engine and carved away enough of the inner fenders to fit the exhaust headers. I also hogged out the rusted and bent rear wheel openings to make room for larger tires using a template designed by the kids, and I welded in patches to repair the rusted areas behind the rear wheels. When they returned in January they installed the engine, transmission, radiator, and headers.

The first semester was quickly coming to a close and several of them would be completing the program. Because they'd worked so hard I vowed that we would have the car running before they left. On a Monday in late January, Rusty rumbled to life! After we set the timing by ear and topped off the fluids I backed the car outside and drove it back and forth across the parking lot. With each jab of the accelerator Rusty leaped, but in a school setting I had to refrain from spinning the tires even though there was little doubt the car was capable of doing so. Later that afternoon, I found that putting down more than sixty feet of rubber from a roll was effortless.

We had another project car that was powered by a stock Chevy 305 with open headers. Running that car in the shop didn't bother any of the other classes, but Rusty's bark was louder and raspier than the Chevy's. I got complaints from the teachers of two other classes. It seems their students feared the car was about to burst through the block wall and into their classrooms!

As the spring semester got underway and new students entered the program we continued our work. I repaired the rusted fenders and the students installed them. We also updated the ignition system with a more modern electronic setup, installed a tachometer, mounted a pair of slightly used drag radial tires on the rear, and addressed many other small details. Unfortunately, we don't have an auto body program, so the paint and bodywork would have to wait. Although Rusty wasn't pretty, I promised the students that if all went well, we would see the drag strip before the end of the school year.

On the first Friday night in May we loaded Rusty onto the same tow dolly I'd used to transport it to school nearly three years earlier. Later that afternoon we headed to Cecil County Dragway near Northeast, Maryland for a couple of shakedown runs. Despite a soft launch due to the torque converter not being matched to our application, I piloted Rusty through the quarter mile from a standing start in 13.2 seconds, crossing the finish line at 105 miles per hour. The kids were ecstatic!

There is plenty of room for improvement and the students realize that Rusty may never be completely finished, but they've seen firsthand how hard work and ingenuity can pay huge dividends even when working with a small budget. For just a couple thousand dollars we've posted performance numbers that many fail to achieve after spending ten times as much. More important, the students have also seen much of the theory we've covered in the classroom come to life.

Despite being a budget build, I spent a substantial amount of time and money on this project, but it was my students who were the true motivation behind it. If not for their protest to my original plan we would have relieved this car of its usable parts and sent it to the crusher. Furthermore, I would have believed that in reclaiming and preserving those parts, we had done a good thing. But considering Rusty's two possible fates, clearly one had a greater potential for positive impact on the futures of our students. The kids were right. Sometimes a change of plans is best!

Sharing Our Passion with the Older Generation

Another birthday has recently come and gone. Although I am not bothered by the fact that each year seems to pass faster than the previous one, I would be remiss if I didn't take a moment to reflect on where I am on life's timeline. Of course, none of us knows how far our own timelines will extend, but I think it's a sure bet that I am well beyond the midpoint of my own timeline. Inexplicably and unwittingly, more than a decade ago I somehow managed to sidestep any midlife crisis that might have come my way. Perhaps that's an indication of inner peace and acceptance of my lot in life, even if it didn't seem that way at the time.

As I reflect on the years that have passed and take note of where I am today, I am fortunate to have few regrets. Life has never been easy, and I have endured my share of setbacks, but I am grateful for the experiences that have shaped and tempered me, the opportunities that have come my way, and the wonderful people who have made my years so rich with memories. Despite my charge-ahead nature, life has, for the most part, ignored my plans. Thinking back to the vision of the future I held more than thirty years ago, I am not at all where I thought I would be. For that I am glad, because I now realize that despite my efforts to the contrary, somehow I have wound up exactly where I belong.

Of course, automobiles have comprised the very fiber of my being from my earliest days. Cars have been my hobby since I was a teen, and all three of the careers that I have enjoyed have been directly linked to them. The world of automobiles has also brought me into contact with countless like-minded individuals. Scrolling through my list of Facebook friends, nearly all of our connections were made through cars.

When I was a young man, I cruised Main Street in Newark, Delaware until it became more of a social happening than a car-lover's mecca. I also frequented what might have been the first cruise spot in the area at The Porch restaurant in New Castle, Delaware. The car shows that I attended were always focused on the cars, and that held true as other cruises, such as the Fox Run Shopping Center cruise, sprang up more than a quarter of a century ago.

Lately, however, I have observed a shift. Maybe it's because I'm getting older; maybe it's because we are all getting older. Recently I took my two older grandsons (ages 9 and 11) to the Soul Riders' car club show at the Hearth Restaurant in Odessa, Delaware. We arrived late and mingled with the folks in the parking lot. Only when the day drew to a close did it occur to me that we hadn't made the rounds to see all of the cars present. Not looking at all of the cars would have bothered me when I was a younger man. Today, however, I see it differently. Mingling with friends means more to me than seeing every car that shows up.

It is our vehicles that bring the members of our community together, but the relationships and friendships we forge are what bind us for life. As our timelines finally do run out one by one, it is heartwarming to see friends pay tribute to those who have passed by attending the services in their special vehicles. Yet, I see another trend. Nearly all of us became "car people" during our formative years as a result of a particularly strong memory involving a particular car. Because cars are an integral part of our daily lives, nearly everyone has memories of a certain car even if those memories failed to ignite the automotive passion within them. In recent months I have seen several accounts of children tracking down the car (or one similar to it) that their fathers drove when they were young men. The children secretly purchase the car, restore it if necessary, and then present it to their father. Such stories are rife with emotion, usually evoking tears from the old men and the grown children alike.

During the years my parents dated, my father had a '57 Plymouth Belvedere, which he later traded for a '57 Fury. Although he had the Fury for less than a year, the memories he made with that car could fill a lifetime. Being in college at the time, when the transmission began to fail, he traded it on a nearly new fuel efficient '60 Corvair. It was this car that he drove back and forth from my grandparents' home in Salisbury, Maryland to school in North Carolina and to visit my mother in Wilmington, Delaware. It was also this car that my parents drove as they began their life together as a married couple.

In the fall of 1977, when I was twelve, my father spied a '63 Corvair 700 coupe on a local used car lot. Its maroon paint had been overtaken by surface rust, but it had low mileage and it ran quite well. I remember him discussing it with my mother. To her chagrin, he bought it. The plan was for it to become a father-son project, but that never happened. Two years later, they traded it in for a new Volkswagen Rabbit. I was heartbroken, and I think to some degree my father was too. I am now much older and wiser than he was at the time. Today I realize that, "I don't care. Do whatever you want!" was merely an expression of exasperation and not at all the approval for purchase that he had taken it to be.

During the four decades since then, I have harbored a desire for a first generation Corvair coupe. My father's '63 coupe had the base engine with a Powerglide two-speed automatic transmission. Admittedly, it was a slug compared to his friend Randy's '64 Monza coupe with a 110 HP engine and four-speed manual transmission. Although I have always been a "Mopar guy," the want for a Corvair persisted.

More than a year ago I began perusing Corvair ads. It was my goal to take my father for a ride in an early model Corvair coupe while I still had the chance. It's not that I thought Dad was going anywhere anytime soon, but one never knows about these things. He hadn't driven in many years, so presenting him with a Corvair of his own was no longer an option. This would be my car, but one that we would enjoy together. As I learned about these cars, I decided that a '64 was the year I most desired. That was the last year of the early body style, but the '64 models received a bump in engine displacement as well as a somewhat improved suspension.

On a springtime Monday morning I spotted a '64 Spyder on eBay. The Spyder is the turbocharged version, which didn't interest me, but the rest of the car looked great, and it had a four-speed. More important, my wife said, "I like the color. Buy it!" I clicked the Buy It Now and left the mandatory deposit.

If it seems too good to be true, it probably is—that old adage echoed in my mind when I went to fork over the remainder of the cash and pick up my new purchase. The car was not as described and there are some underlying issues that had not been disclosed. Clearly, the seller and I had different definitions of the term rust-free. I could have walked away and forfeited my deposit, but I didn't. Is the car worth what I paid? Probably not, but, I also knew that I would have to invest more into a lesser car to bring it to a comparable condition. Furthermore, I could make this car roadworthy quickly. I weighed each of these thoughts while looking the car over, but then it occurred to me that my real motivation in obtaining this car couldn't be evaluated by an appraiser or a collector car price guide. Purchasing this particular car might not be a wise decision from a monetary standpoint, but I felt that it was the right decision considering my circumstances.

In the weeks that followed, I made a number of minor repairs and tracked down several parts that were either damaged or missing. Then, on Father's Day weekend, I drove the Corvair to my parents' home. They both raved over the little coupe. Although my mother never cared for my father's '63 coupe, she had fond memories of his first Corvair. Later in the day I took my father for a ten-mile jaunt to my sister's place for dinner. The whole way he gushed about his memories of the '60 model he had owned more than 50 years prior.

I wanted to share this car with my father often, but he has ridden in it only once. Having suffered multiple strokes, it was too difficult and painful for him to enter and exit the car due to its low stance. With that in mind, I haven't decided if we will keep it indefinitely. It turns out that my wife is rather indifferent about the little coupe. While I really like it and enjoy driving it, I'm not sure that it really fits me. As a close friend once said about a Chevelle that he kept for only a short time, "I bought it, but I never moved in." Even if we take a bath on this car, I will not regret buying it. Some things are more important than money, and my father's excitement was worth far more than any monetary loss we might suffer. I know he won't be around forever, and seeing his joy, I know the money was well spent.

Sometimes, Letting Go Is the Right Choice

To many high-performance car enthusiasts in northern Delaware, Bryan Rash needs no introduction. He has raced often at Cecil County Dragway in nearby Rising Sun, Maryland for decades, and he has presided over two local car clubs, Blue Diamond Classic Chevys and Cruisers for Christ Christian Car Club. In addition, he managed the NuCar Chevrolet Performance Center from its beginning in 1991 until 2006, and he has owned and managed his own auto repair shop, Peak Performance Automotive in Newark, Delaware since 2009. In addition to his automotive endeavors, he is a devoted husband and family man.

Under his leadership, the Cruisers for Christ Christian Car Club hosted car shows at local churches in Delaware, but it also repaired and donated cars to families in need. Bryan said, "This was one of the most rewarding times in my life."

When asked where his automotive passion began, he explained, "I was really young at the time when my cousin had a '73 Camaro. It was a four-speed, and it had side pipes and air shocks. I used to love riding with him in that car. He also gave me all of his hand-me-down car magazines, and I would read them from cover to cover. I would read anything I could get my hands on as long as it had to do with cars."

Like many of us, his earliest days behind the wheel included unsanctioned acceleration trials on public roads in his first car. In his case, that car was a '69 Chevelle. Late one night, while racing on Kirkwood Highway, the engine expired in a hail of broken metal bits. "I put several holes in the block. Only three pistons were still connected to the crankshaft, and the oil pan was full of piston skirts," Bryan said. Soon, he put together another engine, a 350 with strong internals, and he resumed his illicit late-night activities.

Bryan attended the Automotive Training Center in Exton, Pennsylvania from 1981 until 1983, when he graduated. While enrolled there, he met his wife, Heather, who was still in high school. After graduation, they traveled to Arizona together to visit her mother. "We got engaged at the Philadelphia airport," Bryan said. Arizona agreed with the young couple, and they decided to relocate there. "We stayed with her mom for a month. Then, within a week, we got married, found an apartment, I found a job, and she got signed up for college." At the time, Bryan was 20 and Heather was 19. "We got married on my lunch hour. Since I had just started a new job, I didn't feel right asking for time off. We have now been married for almost 39 years."

Eventually, the couple moved back to Delaware. "I started working at NuCar Chevrolet in 1988. In 1991, the NuCar Performance Center opened, and I managed it for the next fifteen years." He also worked on the pit crew of dealership owner Dave Greytak's blown, nitro-burning '38 Chevy coupe. During this time, he always had a project or two going in his shop at home, and his work at the Performance Center kept him well connected with other local car owners, builders, and racers. One day he met with a customer who had a '67 Chevy II project car. "He was having problems with the clutch not disengaging. I took a look at it and discovered that the Z-bar was cracked. It was flexing, and not activating the clutch fork." The two struck up a deal, and the Chevy II moved to Bryan's possession in exchange for his '63 Corvette convertible project car. The Chevy II had a solid body, good interior, and nice paint, but it was sold without an engine or rear axle.

Heather was on board with this latest build. "She grew up around cars. Her father owned Shadetree Automotive." Located in Marshallton, Delaware, Shadetree Automotive has specialized in imports for more than forty years. Heather has also owned a few fast cars of her own, including a Torch Red '96 Z-28 with a six-speed manual transmission.

Bryan built the Chevy II to his liking. He installed a twelve-bolt rear axle, initially outfitted with a 4.10 ratio. The 4.10s soon gave way to 4.30s, and then to 4.56s. "The 4.56s worked the best. Eventually I added a spool," Brian said. Inside, he added an eight-point roll bar and five-point safety harnesses for the front seat occupants. It already had a Muncie four-speed transmission. For motivation, he started with a 350 block and had its cylinders bored 0.030-inch oversize. Then he filled it with good internals including Keith Black hypereutectic pistons, LT1 powdered rods with ARP bolts, a forged steel crankshaft, and a .595/.596 lift hydraulic roller camshaft. "I used an Air Flow Research 'Rev Kit,' which helped to control the motion of the heavy hydraulic roller lifters without putting additional load on the plungers, pushrods, or rocker arms," Bryan explained. "It put an additional thirty pounds of pressure on the lifter bodies."

Of course, the initial build is just the starting point. After that comes a period of tuning and tweaking the combination for optimum performance. "I went through three sets of leaf springs just to get the stance right," Bryan said. "After that, I tuned the slapper bars by using urethane bumpers and shimming them with washers." He also switched carburetors to an AED brand Eliminator model, which was based on a Holley 650 CFM carburetor, but used an 850 CFM throttle plate. The small venturis were blended to match the large throttle bores. The result was a carburetor that provided excellent low and mid-range response, as well as great high-speed power due to its 830 CFM of air flow. Ultimately, the Chevy II posted quarter mile times of 11.60 seconds at 119 miles per hour. "The launches with that carburetor were incredible! The sixty-foot time dropped to 1.5 seconds. I launched it at 5200 RPM and shifted at 7,000. But the best thing about it was that you could jump in it at any time and take it for a ride. My wife and I drove it (approximately 100 miles each way) to both the spring and fall cruises in Ocean City, Maryland for about three years. It drove well on the street."

The hard launches associated with drag racing tend to reveal any weak parts in a drivetrain, and that was true of both the custom aluminum driveshaft and the Muncie transmission. After destroying three Muncie four-speeds, Bryan contacted Liberty's Gears, Inc. "They built me a transmission that used a Borg Warner Super T-10 case with all good gears and such. That transmission held up well." The clutch also proved to be problematic due to the high RPM launches. After experimenting unsuccessfully with several different brands, Bryan discovered that a Centerforce pressure plate paired with a Hayes disc provided the durability he needed for racing as well as the street manners he sought. "I had the car set up so that I could remove the transmission in about twenty minutes. Replacing the clutch took about an hour from start to finish. I would replace the clutch once every year, and I had no other trouble with it."

Meanwhile, the Rashes wanted to start a family. Working through an adoption agency, they assembled a portfolio intended to provide prospective birth mothers with some insight about who they were. By reviewing the portfolios of numerous couples, a birth mother could narrow her choices and ultimately choose which couple she felt most comfortable with raising her child. "For one mother, it finally came down to another couple and us. But when she looked at the pictures we had provided, she chose us." Those pictures were of Bryan and Heather standing in front of the Chevy II, which was still under construction. "When she saw the car, she knew she wanted us to raise her son." As the pregnancy progressed, the Rashes remained involved. "Heather went to the doctor's appointments with the birth mother. When Ryan was born, we were there, and we brought him home from the hospital."

Bryan added another harness to the rear seat of the Chevy II which secured Ryan's car seat. "He loved riding in the car as long as we were moving. Whenever we stopped at a traffic light, he would cry. But when the light turned green and we started moving again, he would laugh."

Six years later, they adopted a two-year old girl named Amy. "A woman in our church had a sister who had been involved in a serious car accident and was in a coma. The woman was a single mom who had kids of her own, and the added pressure of looking after her sister's kids was just too much for her. She asked for help from the church members. We agreed to babysit Amy for an extended time, which eventually led to our adopting her. It took four years for the adoption to be finalized.

"Adoption is expensive, especially if you work through an adoption agency," Bryan said. "The Chevy II helped us to adopt our son, but it also helped us to adopt our daughter. I sold it in order to raise the money we needed to pay for the adoption. So really, the car helped us to adopt both kids and to create our family."

Today, Ryan and Amy are twenty-two and seventeen respectively. "Ryan enjoys sports, and he plays football and basketball. Although he doesn't enjoy getting his hands greasy, he has a need for speed, just like I do. His first car was a Murray Dip Side pedal car, which came as an unpainted, disassembled kit." Father and son built it and had it professionally painted by the NuCar Chevrolet body shop. "It was professionally painted to match Dave Greytak's racecar—white with flames, and Viper Red inside." The headlights and other details were painted by local pinstriper and custom painter Angel Cruz.

"Amy is hell on wheels, whether she's on an ATV or anything else! She used to ride on the back of my Harley from the time she was eight years old, and she was really upset when I sold it. Nowadays she loves going to Cecil County Dragway, either with us or with her friends. I get jealous whenever she goes without us," Bryan laughed. He describes her as a driven young woman who pushes herself to excel, and who has her sights set on the military. "She's a straight-A student, and she works out in the gym for two hours a day because she wants to be fit when she goes to boot camp."

Today, the Rash family is still building cars. Currently, Bryan is building a '64 Nova resto-mod for a customer in his shop at home, and he has a '99 Jeep of his own waiting for his attention. In the meantime, he and Amy are building a '95 Jeep for her. "She has done a considerable amount of the work in putting her Jeep together. She replaced the fuel tank, installed the lift kit, and coated the inside with liquid bed liner. She is chomping at the bit for me to turn it over to her."

The Rashes are devout in their Christian beliefs, but it was an experience during a Father's Day car show at Iron Hill Community Church in New Castle that drew Bryan back to his faith in God. Having been away from the church for about twenty years, he explained, "The Lord stirred something in me that day."

Although the Rashes' Chevy II is gone, the role it played in their family cannot be overstated. Consequently, it will long hold its place in their hearts.

Sometimes the Sequel Surpasses the Original

Bill Berry named his '68 Road Runner "Fine Lee" for two reasons. "My wife's name is Leta, but everyone calls her Lee." Therefore, it is a play on her name. "It also means 'Finally,' because it took sixteen years to make it drivable."

Bill grew up on a farm in western Pennsylvania. "There were Chrysler products in my family before me. My father had a '48 Plymouth, and I've got a picture of me standing in front of it when I was two years old. We lived in a valley, and on my first ride in that car, we were heading uphill in snow when the car did a donut!

"My first car was a '64 Plymouth Savoy coupe with a 318. I bought it in 1966, and I didn't have it a month before I wrecked it. I hadn't even made the first payment!" The accident involved heavy fog, a curve, a ditch with a log in it, and the swamp beyond the ditch where the car came to a rest. "I was on my way home from visiting Leta. We were going together then, and I <u>might</u> have fallen asleep." The left fender and door were heavily damaged, as was the B-pillar post. Bill had a wrecker retrieve his Plymouth from the swamp and he parked it in the back yard behind his family's house.

"Leta and I got engaged in '67, and in '68 I was in Vietnam. She kept sending me pictures and advertisements for the '68 Chrysler cars, which included Road Runners, GTXs, and Barracudas. While I was over there, I sent money home, and about a month before I came home, my father took my Savoy to a shop to have it fixed. It was a light blue car, and a buddy of mine painted it burgundy. On the day Leta and I got married, it was 65 degrees. At the wedding, they decorated the car with streamers and tape. We went to Niagara Falls on our honeymoon, and the next morning, the car was covered in ice. I started to remove the tape, and it took the maroon paint with it. So, then we had a burgundy car with blue stripes."

By 1969 the couple had settled in western New York. Bill was working for Marlin Rockwell, a bearing manufacturer that was later acquired by bearing giant SKF. "Leta worked for Faulkner Glass during the day, and I worked second shift. I had the car when she was at work, and she had the car when I was at work. I would meet her for lunch. One day I spotted an orange Road Runner on the Plymouth dealer's lot. I went in and talked to them, and they told me what I'd get for trade-in on my Savoy. The payment was 109 dollars a month. I signed the papers, and I drove it to meet Leta at noon. When she came outside, she didn't see the Savoy. I beeped the horn and she came over. She asked, 'Are you taking it for a test drive?' I said, 'Nope. We bought it.'" Bill and Leta's Road Runner had the basic 383 and automatic transmission powertrain. "It had big hubcaps and red sidewalls. I bought grayish colored five-spoke mags and different tires, and I saved the original wheels and tires."

"That was MY Road Runner!" Leta said.

"Leta is a daredevil driver." Bill chuckled. "She dropped me off at work one Saturday, and then she went home to sun herself. When she came to pick me up, she had lotion on her hands. She was going around a curve when a dump truck came from the other direction, half-way on her side of the road. She swerved to miss the truck, and she got the car up on two wheels! The lady who lived in the house where it happened said she saw the bottom of the car."

Unfortunately, the Road Runner did not stay in Bill and Leta's possession for long. "We only had it for seven months when I got laid off. We couldn't afford to keep the house and the car, so we had to let the car go," Bill said. Making matters worse, the Road Runner's second owner was a woman named Mabel, with whom Bill worked. Every day he was tortured by seeing it parked in the lot outside his shop. Even so, it was a wise choice, for Bill and Leta still live in the same home that they purchased as newlyweds. The payment on the Road Runner had been higher than their monthly mortgage payment, so they replaced it with a '70 Duster 340, which was followed by a '72 Duster. As the years rolled by, several Ramchargers also passed through their hands. Still, they missed their Road Runner. One day Bill declared, "I will have another one before I turn fifty."

In 1996, one month before his fiftieth birthday, a blue '68 Road Runner came up for sale locally. Originally equipped with a 383 and a four-speed transmission, a non-running 440 and an automatic transmission now resided in their place. Bill's daughter, Amy Bragg, is no stranger to cars. She graduated from an auto body and refinishing program when she was in high school, so she went with Bill to examine the car. "Amy and I looked it over. She crawled around underneath to make sure it was solid." The asking price was a paltry two-thousand dollars, so Bill ran home to get the money and his tow bar. "Amy steered it while I towed it home. When my wife saw it she said, 'You're crazy! You bought a car and you don't even know if it runs?' I said, 'Yes, but even not running it's worth twice what I paid for it.'"

What Leta saw was a tired looking car with its tattered headliner hanging down, no carpet, and mis-matched bucket seats from a Charger in place of the original bench seat. Dingy slotted wheels with missing center caps had long ago replaced the originals. "The radio, ash tray, and side marker lights were all in the trunk." Undaunted, Bill removed the battery from his truck and connected it to the Road Runner. He trickled fuel down the throat of the carburetor, and to his delight the 440 started immediately. "It quit after a few seconds, but I put fuel into the gas tank and a little more down the carburetor, and it ran just fine after that."

Bill and Leta don't have a garage. "We put it in her (Leta's) mother's garage. Right after that, I was diagnosed with kidney cancer. After I was done with that, Leta was diagnosed with breast cancer. The car sat in her mother's garage for fifteen years, until she passed away." The Road Runner was temporarily stored elsewhere before being moved into Amy's barn.

"I've got an old grain barn that is over a hundred years old. It was built with peg and beam construction, and it has a heavy wood plank floor," Amy said. "It's cold storage, but the car is out of the weather." Despite its age, the barn is in fantastic condition, and it is located in her back yard. Bill and Leta's house is mere minutes away.

Work on the Road Runner began in earnest once it moved to Amy's barn. Bill installed a new headliner and new carpet. Because the original transmission was a four-speed, there was no factory shifter on the column or the floor for the automatic transmission. Instead, an aftermarket ratchet shifter had been bolted to the floor hump by a previous owner. To replace the carpet, Bill had to remove the shifter, and then reinstall it. "I had the car jacked up so I could get under it. Two of the bolts for the shifter went through the floor right above the driveshaft. I set the shifter in place and put the bolts through the holes, but every time I tried to reach above the driveshaft and start the nuts, I knocked the bolts out of their holes. Back and forth under the car, I got splinters in my back from the wood floor. Finally, I had to have Leta come out and hold the bolts so I could get the nuts started." Bill also purchased new factory style seat upholstery. In place of the Charger bucket seats, he installed a bench seat. "A guy down near Pittsburgh had it, and he only wanted 125 dollars for it.

I had a local guy put the new upholstery on, and he charged me 75 dollars per seat." Bill also purchased a set of Magnum 500 style wheels (Road Wheels in Chrysler parlance) and a set of BF Goodrich radial tires.

By 2011 Bill was finally behind the wheel of a Road Runner once more, and he is happy to share it with his daughter. "Amy is the only one of our kids who has expressed any interest in it. When I get to the point that I can't drive it anymore, it'll become hers."

"Hopefully before I turn fifty!" Amy quipped.

Bill laughed. "Yeah, she's trying to figure out how to keep me from driving it."

Since resurrecting the long dormant car, Bill has visited its former owner a couple of times. "When I bought it, he was a young guy, maybe twenty-eight. He and his wife needed the money to buy a house. The first time I went back to visit, they had bought a nice little home, and their son was small. When I went back the last time, their son was much older. When he saw the car, I guess he thought about how cool it would be to drive it to school. He looked at is dad and said, 'you were an idiot!'"

In comparing his two Road Runners, Bill said, "When we had the orange car, we used it for daily life. This one has become more of a show car. I meet people with it. I meet all kinds of different people. It's not there for work purposes. It's there for pleasure." Although very presentable, the car is not without blemishes, and that seems to suit Bill just fine. "I'm not afraid of going to Wal-Mart and having somebody open a door into it or getting a stone chip. I drive it about 3,000 miles a year."

Bill, Leta, and Amy all enjoy participating in car shows in their area. In addition, Bill and Amy have participated in the All Chrysler Nationals in Carlisle, Pennsylvania for the last five years. 2018 was the 50th year celebration of the 1968 models at Carlisle, and the Road Runner garnered a Celebrity Pick award. In addition, their car was one of the half-dozen chosen to be displayed outside of the banquet hall where that year's Mopar Hall of Fame inductions took place. Bob Laravee and Bill Moeller, creators of the Plymouth Rapid Tansit System Caravan, were among the inductees.

The Plymouth Rapid Transit System Caravan was a carnival-like affair that traveled the country, moving from one Plymouth dealership to the next in order to draw attention to the marque's high-performance cars during the 1970 and 1971 model years. The display featured customized Road Runner, Duster, and Barracuda cars. In 1970, Bill had photographed the show cars, including Don "The Snake" Prudhomme's Barracuda funny car drag racer, at a dealership in Jamestown, New York. Now, nearly fifty years later, he had brought that photo with him. That evening he met the two men responsible for the traveling display, and they autographed his photo.

Last fall, Amy and her fiancé Jeff Hosier planned a trip, but they did not disclose their destination to Bill or Leta. They loaded the Road Runner onto a trailer, and then they picked up Bill and Leta at their house. Their secret destination was the Ridgely Car Show, hosted by Brenda Walls in Ridgely, Maryland, a sleepy town on Maryland's eastern shore. Although Ridgely is an unlikely location for a major event, the show has featured numerous celebrities in the automotive realm, including Linda Vaughn and NASCAR legend Richard Petty. "I got to meet my stock car hero, and he signed my glovebox," Bill said.

While they trailered the Road Runner to the most recent Carlisle and Ridgely shows, Bill and Amy drove it to Carlisle for the first four years that they attended, and during that time they shared some adventures. Bill said, "The first year we went, I had replaced the windshield wiper motor ahead of time. We had wipers, but the heater core was leaking, so I had it bypassed. The defroster wasn't working, so while I drove, Amy sat with a roll of paper towels, and she had to keep wiping the insides of the windows so I could see at eighty miles per hour."

"We lost a tailpipe the next year. It rotted off right behind the muffler," Amy said. On another trip a rear axle bearing failed. In 2020, electrical and fuel pump issues plagued them for the entire trip. That was the first year that Jeff had joined them. Amy said, "No matter what, she always gets us home."

Although Fine Lee's revival was delayed, Bill Berry and his family have been making up for lost time ever since.

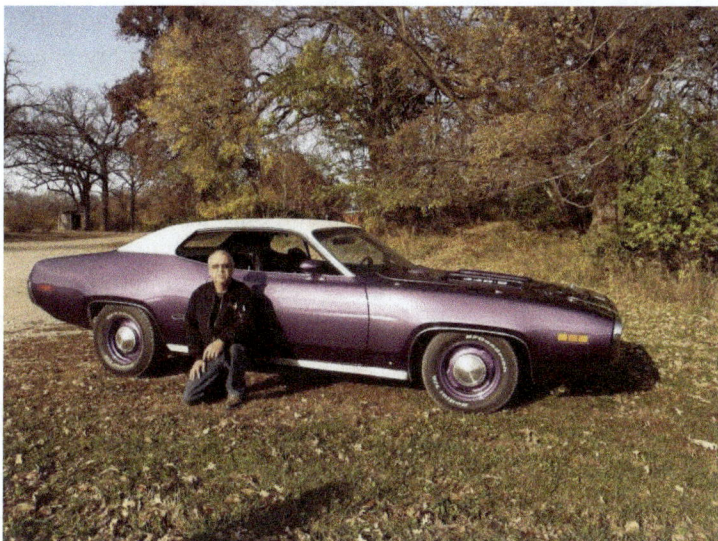

The Making of the Beast

The story of Randy Lowe's '71 Plymouth actually begins with the car he had owned prior to it. "I had a '70 V-code Road Runner," Randy said. The "V" in the fifth digit of the Vehicle Identification Number indicated that his Road Runner had been built with a 440 cubic inch V-8 engine with three two-barrel carburetors and a rating of 390 horsepower. "I was twenty years old. I didn't know much about Mopar muscle cars, but I knew that I liked them. My car was Winchester Gray, and it had a four-speed and a Dana 60 rear axle. It had regular drum brakes, regular manual steering, and no radio. It was meant to go in a straight line really fast, and it did that well. Handling and stopping? Not so much." Due to the harsh Iowa winters, by 1974 the quarter panels and rocker panels were already showing heavy rust. "It would be a very special car today, and it would be considered an easy restoration because the replacement metal is available. But back then it was just a car, and parts were not available to fix it."

"A friend bought a '71 Plymouth Satellite Sebring Plus, and I really liked it. It was purple with a white vinyl top, a black and white hounds tooth bucket seat interior, and a 383 motor. He couldn't afford the payments, and he was about to lose it. I had just put a bunch of money into my 440. I said, 'Let's trade cars, but keep our own motors.' One weekend we did a motor swap between the two cars." Fortunately, the crankshaft of the 383 was drilled for a pilot bushing, which was necessary with the four-speed transmission in the Road Runner.

"The Satellite was our daily driver. Being a family car, my wife Cheri drove it as much as I did, and our kids rode in it often. That was a

financially good year, so I ordered a new Monte Carlo. It had a 454 V-8, a
Turbo Hydramatic 400 transmission, an eight-track tape player, a sunroof,
and swivel bucket seats. I dressed it up to the tune of 5400 dollars. That
was our second car, and we thought we had two good daily driver cars.
That big block Chevy was a piece of shit! It always burned oil. The carpet
and headliner were also crooked. It really was a lemon." After a few years,
the Lowe family moved out of Waterloo and onto some acreage outside of
town. Randy said, "After we moved, I parked the Monte Carlo. Eventually
I traded it for two new chainsaws. But now I was commuting a hundred
miles a day in the Satellite. With rising gas prices, I pulled out the 440 and
installed a 318. Then it was affordable to drive."

What the 318 offered in economy it lacked in performance.
Consequently, Randy often swapped between the two engines. "I had pins
made for the motor mounts, which made it easy to change motors. I could
pull the small block and put in the big block in a few hours, and then I had
a hot-rod again. I had a separate driveshaft made, and the engine and
transmission stayed together.

"I had to leave for work very early in the morning. During the
winter, I would start the car and let it warm up. One morning, after letting
it warm up, I went outside to leave for work, but the car wasn't in the
driveway. We had eleven acres of woods around us, and I could see the
lights shining in the woods. The shifter had slipped out of park and the car
had idled across the yard, idled across our garden, and idled into the woods
until it bumped into a tree. Luckily it didn't do any damage."

On another winter morning, Cheri drove their kids to school.
Randy said, "It was twenty miles round-trip, and it was a zero-degree day.
It seemed that things always happened in the wintertime. When Cheri got
home, she said the car was overheated, so I checked it. The belts were on,
but I could hear the engine gurgling. The engine was hot, but the radiator
was frozen solid. Apparently, I didn't have enough anti-freeze in it. Those
318s are so forgiving! Once it cooled off, it ran just like it always did.

"On another snowy cold day, Cheri and a friend decided to go
shopping in Cedar Rapids, which is sixty miles away. The two of them and
our daughters piled into the car and left for the trip. Halfway home, they
windowed the block." When an engine suffers a connecting rod failure, the
half of the rod that remains attached to the crankshaft is swung around the
crankshaft as it rotates. It can collide violently with the oil pan and the
sides of the engine block, often punching holes through them. These holes
are commonly referred to as windows. "In white-out conditions, nobody
would stop at first. Of course, there were no cell phones then. Finally,
somebody stopped and gave them a ride to town. They called me, and I
went and picked them up.

"During another winter, I was in a bar in Cedar Falls, which was
fifty to fifty-five miles away. A very drunk young lady needed a ride home

about four blocks away, so I offered to take her there. After we left the bar, she said she had bought a T-shirt there, and she had left it behind. I drove back to the bar, and I ran inside to get the shirt. When I came back out, she and the car were gone! The police found it the next morning half a block from the police station. The doors were locked, and the engine was idling. It looked like she had gone down a narrow alley and pinballed off some dumpsters. Both sides were banged up and the mirrors were ripped off.

"That wasn't the only time it was stolen. I had an electrical contracting business, and I had to drop off some paperwork at my partner's home. Living in the country, back then we left our keys in our cars and we didn't lock our houses. We really didn't think about it because we didn't have problems with crime. But I was at my partner's for no more than five minutes. I came outside, and the car wasn't there. I called the police, and they found it half an hour later. It was parked in a housing project in Waterloo. The keys were still in it, and it had no damage.

On another cold Iowa winter morning in 1984, I was driving to work at five-thirty in the morning. I was running late, so I was roaring down Highway Three, which is a perfectly straight road, and I was doing about eighty. A big buck walked from the ditch and out into the road, and he stood right in front of me. I had no choice but to hit it. He came over the hood and into the windshield. One antler punched a perfectly round hole in the left front fender. He rolled into the ditch on the opposite side of the road. He destroyed the front of my car, but we got 120 pounds of meat out of him.

"It took a couple of weekends to make the car drivable again. It wasn't pretty, but it was drivable. After that, I parked it in the woods thinking, 'Someday I'm going to fix it up.' When we moved back to Waterloo in 1987, the city had just passed an ordinance stating that all cars parked outside a residence must be licensed and operable. I was going to crush the car, but my friends talked me out of it. So, I put it behind our house. If someone bitched about it, they bitched. But no one ever did. While it was there, the kids used to climb on it and pretend to drive it.

"It was our family car. It was a pretty car, but nothing special. It was our daily go to the grocery store, drop the kids off at school car. It was cool, but as far as I knew it didn't have any other value. But I liked the car!

"A friend had a parts car in 1999, and I wanted all of the bright work from it. He offered me the whole car for what he wanted for just the bright work. I bought it, and I'm glad I did. I ended up using both doors, one fender, wiring, and more. A few years later, I sold the rest of the parts car for more than I paid for it. Fast forward to now, the parts car is under restoration by the new owner.

"In 2002 I finally decided it was time to restore our Satellite. We pulled the 318 and started tearing it down. I had arranged for it to go into a body shop about forty miles away that was known for doing really good

Mopar restorations. I knew it would be there for a couple of years. It was supposed to go in on a Monday, but I had heart issues on the Friday before. I wound up in the hospital for four bypasses, but they couldn't do the surgery until the following week. I lived half a mile from the hospital, and I wanted to go home and finish prepping the car for its trip to the body shop, but the doctor wouldn't let me leave. I said I was going to leave anyway, but then my wife took all of my clothes so I couldn't leave. I had four bypasses on Monday, and the body shop arranged to pick up the car that day."

During the 1971 model year, the only family sized Plymouths that were available with the 440 Six Barrel engine were the Road Runner and the upscale GTX, both of which were high performance models. Being a Satellite Sebring Plus, Randy's car was an upscale model like the GTX, and since the 440 had resided in it for so much of its life, he decided to add the hood, rear valence, and remaining trim pieces to replicate a GTX. In addition, it needed both quarter panels and a new floor, which were sourced from donor cars in Oregon.

Many body shops avoid restoration work. Those that do restorations often use such jobs as filler work between collision jobs. "Two years turned into three, and three years turned into four. Finally, the owner of the body shop said he'd give it back to us to install the drivetrain, and then he would finish the outside. We did that, and then we took it back. One year went by. Then another year started going by. I had been stopping in periodically to check on the progress, but then I started getting excuses for why I couldn't go by. I just knew something was up. Where do you go in a small town to get information? To the bar! So, I went and I asked if anybody knew about a purple GTX at this particular body shop. One guy said it was being stored in the owner's barn at his home. He was working on a triple black Hemi Challenger or Barracuda instead. I had to get a lawyer involved. The car was a mess, but he did finish it. It looks good, though it has flaws. But the body work he did was impeccable! There is no evidence inside or outside that he put two quarter panels on it."

After the Plymouth was returned to the Lowes, Randy and his son Andrew chipped away at it over the next several years. "The restoration took twelve years. It seemed like twenty, but at that time Cheri and I were raising three kids and paying a mortgage. Still, I would hunt down parts a little at a time. This was before the internet. Once eBay started, it got so much easier!" The same was true of reference material for how the Plymouth had been assembled at the factory. "We would go to car shows, and if I wasn't sure about certain details, I'd take pictures of similar cars and ask questions. It was tough to get information, and even then, it may not be correct.

"A buddy of mine, Bill Miller, installed the headliner and the vinyl top. He did all of that work for a twelve-pack of beer. He was a super guy, the kind of guy you'd want for a friend, but life dealt him the shittiest hand. He had an accident at home, and he passed away before he could see the car finished."

Aside from the body, paint, headliner, and vinyl top, Randy and his son, Andrew, performed the entire restoration at home. Randy explained, "Andrew did the interior pretty much by himself. He and I rebuilt the motor, and it was his first motor rebuild. I did all of the mechanical work with a floor jack and jack stands. I didn't have a lift at the time. During the restoration, I should have replaced the hard plastic front seat backs because my little girls had scratched their initials into them. But you know, that's family history, and I just couldn't bring myself to change them." Along the way, the purple Plymouth assumed the moniker, The Beast.

On Easter Sunday, April 20, 2014 the restoration was finished. "Once it was done, we hit most of the Mopar shows in our area, including Mopars in the Park in Stillwater, Minnesota, Mopars on the Mississippi in Dubuque, Iowa, and the Mopar Happening show in Belvidere, Illinois. In 2019 it was featured at the Mopar Blast in St. Louis, and it was invited to the Muscle Car and Corvette Nationals in Chicago in 2016 and 2018. We also made trips east to the Mopar shows in Carlisle, Pennsylvania in 2017 and 2021." In addition, Randy and Cheri enjoy cruising Fourth Street in Waterloo, where they met five decades ago. "It's a good memory for Cheri and me. It's a good time," Randy said.

While the Plymouth holds countless memories for the Lowe family, which were forged over nearly half a century, today Randy enjoys showing the car. "I like to sit at car shows. I don't walk around much because everyone who comes up has a story, and I like hearing their stories. I know some of them are bullshit, but I still enjoy hearing them. A person who wants to talk may stay for fifteen or twenty minutes, but that's fine with me."

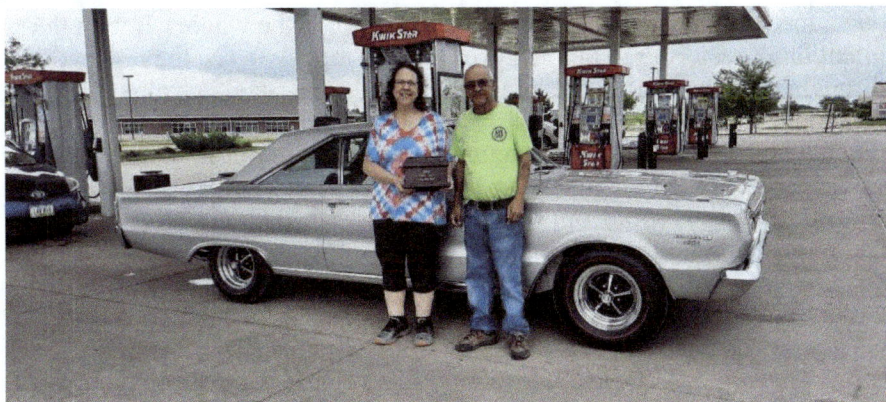

Rebirth of the Silver Fox

It was an autumn afternoon in 2013 when I received an unexpected phone call from my friend, Greg Rager. He asked me, "Are you still looking for a '67 GTX?" I said that I was, and he provided some general information about a GTX located in Kansas City, Missouri. "It's a project, but it's a 440 4-speed, and it's got few options, just the way you like them." Then he gave me Tom Shaw's phone number. Tom's recently deceased brother, Jerry, had owned the car.

Greg is a retired Johnstown, Pennsylvania police officer. In the late 1980s, before he retired, he began writing stories for Muscle Car Review magazine. Upon retiring from police work, he accepted a position with Dobbs Publishing Group, moved to Florida, and became the first technical editor for Muscle Car Review magazine. Larry Dobbs, the president of the company, realized the potential in Greg's vast knowledge of Chrysler vehicles, and quickly launched Mopar Muscle magazine with Greg as the founding editor. It was Greg who gave me my first big break in 1992 when he began publishing my work in Mopar Muscle, and we had remained friends ever since. In April, 1989 Tom Shaw became the editor of Muscle Car Review, and in the years that followed, he and Greg became close friends. Five minutes after they met for the first time in the parking lot at Dobbs Publishing Group, Tom mentioned that his brother, Jerry, owned a '67 GTX. Although Jerry worked for Tom as a freelance photographer from time to time, Greg had met him only once. Now Tom was trying to help Jerry's widow, Rita, place Jerry's car in good hands.

That evening, I spoke with Tom for an hour or more. He had forwarded photos of Jerry's forlorn looking GTX earlier in the day, and he filled in many of the details about the car. Jerry had purchased it in 1978 when he was eighteen years old. Although he had driven it for four years, he had never transferred the title into his name. He said that after it developed engine trouble, Jerry had disassembled the whole car with the intention of restoring it, but he never had the money to see the restoration through. "He also parted out a few Belvederes and Satellites along the way. He would take the best of the parts he had from all of the cars, restore them, and stash them away in an unused bedroom in our father's house. All of the parts to assemble the car are included," Tom said. He also stated that some of the paperwork from when it was purchased by the original owner had remained with the car.

The photos confirmed that the seats and door panels were indeed in a room with many other parts. Smaller pieces, such as the radio and its chrome bezel, had been stashed in the drawers of a file cabinet in the same room. One photo showed the assembly line vehicle build sheet, which had been protected in a plastic sleeve and remained in pristine condition. The transmission was still in the car, but Jerry had removed and disassembled the engine. Many of the mechanical pieces, including the pistons and connecting rods, were in the trunk. Trim pieces were strewn about the barren interior. Rust had pervaded the lower portions of the quarter panels, the rocker panels, and the torsion bar cross member. Although it wore a faded reddish-orange hue on the areas that were not rusted, it had been silver originally. The hood and right fender, however, wore weathered burgundy paint. I asked about the mismatched panels, suspecting that it had been wrecked. Tom laughed. "No, it wasn't wrecked. Jerry had a bit of a temper when he was younger. One day the car refused to start. He got angry, and he beat the fender and hood with a tire iron. Then he had to replace them."

As we talked, it was apparent that Tom was looking out for Rita's interest. He gave me a price which was non-negotiable. In addition, he said, "There is one stipulation. Once it's finished, Rita gets to drive it." I assured him that I would be honored to have her drive Jerry's car. During our conversation I realized that while I was seeking information about the car from Tom, he was interviewing me to determine if I would be a worthy owner and restorer. He asked if I would return it to stock condition, if I would repaint it silver or some other color, and how I would use it. I must have checked all of the right boxes because he gave me Rita's phone number.

The next evening, I called Rita, who confirmed all that Tom had told me. She said that gathering the parts from Jerry's father's house would not be a problem, nor would it be any trouble to obtain the engine block and other large engine pieces from Jerry's friend's garage in Merriam, Kansas. Although one can never be sure when talking to a stranger half a continent away, I had a good feeling when speaking with her.

Over the next week, I made plans with my friend and co-worker Lou Spinelli to travel from Delaware to Missouri to pick up the car and all of its parts. Lou and I both teach Automotive Technology classes at

Delaware Technical Community College. Due to our teaching schedules, we would have to wait until the long Thanksgiving weekend.

A few weeks before Thanksgiving, Rita called me and said, "Frank, I just can't go through with it. It's too soon." Her voice rang with grief. "I hope you're not too disappointed." I had assumed that some months had passed since Jerry's death, but I learned that was not the case. Rita's world had been shattered just weeks earlier, and she hadn't yet begun to pick up the pieces because those pieces were still falling.

I was disappointed, but my disappointment was overshadowed by a sense of solicitude. My heart ached for her. I assured her that I understood. She promised to offer Jerry's GTX to me first should she decide to sell it at a later date. A couple of years later, she made good on that promise. Unfortunately, by then my wife and I had purchased a different GTX, and I knew that we could not afford to restore both cars. Although I wanted Jerry's car, I had to turn down Rita's offer.

Years later, I learned that Jerry and Rita had been married in 1990. "For the first several years, I didn't even know he had a GTX. It had been off the road for many years, and it was sitting at his best friend's place," Rita said. "I never saw it until 1996 when we rented our first house. His friend told him, 'You've got to get this thing out of here.' So, Jerry bought a car cover, and every time we moved after that, it followed us. When we bought our house in 2002, he finally had a garage to store it in. Jerry was a fantastic guitar player, and he had a lot of music equipment, mainly guitars and amplifiers. His music equipment occupied his man cave." Consequently, many of the couple's possessions had been relegated to a storage unit. "About ten years later, we had to empty those things out of our storage unit, so they went into the garage and the car was moved outside. It sat there for a year or two until September 2013 when he died.

"Jerry wanted to restore his car. That had been his plan all along, but we never had the money. I begged him to sell it, but he wouldn't. I didn't realize how much it meant to him. After he died, I looked into restoring it myself as a tribute to him. But then I talked to the owner of a restoration shop, and I could see that the expenses would quickly pile up to fifty thousand dollars or more, which I couldn't afford. So, I made the tough decision to sell it."

In 2016 she listed it for sale in several Facebook groups. Sadly, around Thanksgiving that year Tom Shaw succumbed to his injuries following an automobile accident. The GTX was purchased by Randy Lowe in December. He and his son Andrew moved the car and all of its parts to their home in Buckingham, Iowa later that month.

"Tom died a month or so before I sold it to the Lowes. His sons, Ryan and Austin Shaw, flew up from Florida for Christmas. They were here when the Lowes picked up their Uncle Jerry's car."

Enter Randy and Andrew Lowe:

"When I was nineteen I bought a '65 Belvedere," Randy said. "It was red with a black bench seat interior, and it had a 383 engine and a four-speed transmission. I put a Hurst Competition Plus shifter in it and milled the heads to bump up the compression ratio, and it was just the perfect car. One day I drove into Waterloo to the spot where we used to cruise. I had just finished rubbing out the paint, and it looked good! I was approaching an intersection when a '64 Mercury Comet came from the other direction. Somebody in that car threw a cigarette butt, and it rolled across my hood. I was pissed! I spun a 180 in the middle of the intersection, burned a little rubber, and went after the Comet. I was going to kick someone's ass! I caught up with them and followed them into a parking lot where I boxed them into a parking space. Out of the car came two hot women! So, I married one of them!

"I kept the Belvedere until 1974, at which time I advertised and sold it. By then, my electrical contracting business was going well, and I decided I wanted a new Monte Carlo. I ordered one with a 454 big block V-8, a Turbo Hydramatic 400 transmission, swivel bucket seats, eight-track, and a sunroof. I paid 5400 dollars cash, and it arrived six weeks later. What a piece of shit! The sunroof leaked, it burned oil, and the transmission cooler leaked internally so that it put anti-freeze into the transmission. I was so disgusted that eventually I traded it for two new chainsaws.

"The kid who I sold the Belvedere to brought it back two hours later with a burned-out clutch. I put a new clutch in it for him, and two weeks later, he wrapped it around a utility pole.

"My son, Andrew, knew this story. In 2016 he was looking for another '65 Belvedere like my first one when he found an ad for the GTX. It wasn't a '65, but it had a big block with a four-speed. He showed me the ad, we went down to Rita's that weekend to look at it, and we bought it. When we got home, I said, 'What in the hell have I done?'

"The seats were not in it, but the trunk and inside were full of parts. The front floors were rotted out and the trunk floor was full of rust pinholes. The torsion bar cross member was rotted, and the quarter panels and rockers were gone on both sides. The worst part was that I wasn't familiar with the car. I restored my '71 Plymouth, and I know every bolt and screw in that car, but I had never worked on a '67. I didn't take it apart, so it was like a giant puzzle that I didn't know if I had all of the pieces to."

Randy explained that the first thing he and Andrew did after unloading the car from the trailer and pushing it into their shop was to empty it of its loose parts. "We couldn't fully evaluate the condition of the floors and trunk until we took everything out of the car." They sorted and organized all that they could, but they were unable to identify some trim pieces initially. They took the engine components to a local machine shop to have them reconditioned and the short block assembled, and then they turned their attention to the body.

"I bought rear wheel arch sections that looked like they were hand-formed, but when I laid the wheel opening moldings on them, they fit almost perfectly! I found some of the other metal parts at Auto Metal Direct, and my friend Robert Biretz was able to fabricate the rest. Another friend at the community college where I had worked was able to stamp out new rear bumper mounting reinforcements.

"The first major work we did was to remove the fenders and hood, and we discovered that the right front shock tower needed some work. With the metal repairs, we started at the front and worked our way back. After the shock tower we tackled the floors, torsion bar cross member, rocker panels, quarter panels, and then the cross member where the rear bumper attaches."

After the welding and metal repairs had been completed, Randy had the car blasted with a mixture of glass beads and water to remove the remaining paint and any filler that might have been present from previous body repairs. "We found only two small spots of body filler that had been used to fix a couple of small dents. There were no ugly surprises—no additional rust repairs needed." From the beginning, Randy had planned to send the car to Diamond's Body Shop in Evansdale, Iowa for the finish body work and paint. To protect the bare metal in the meantime, he sprayed on a coat of epoxy primer.

Randy said that while blasting the body panels, he sensed Jerry's presence, as if he was somehow overseeing the progress on his car. "When I mentioned this to Rita, the phone went silent. Then she said, 'Tom's sons and I sprinkled a little bit of Jerry's ashes in the car.'"

Meanwhile, Randy and Andrew made a list of the parts they had and the parts that were missing. They also researched those parts that they could not identify to determine where they belonged. "Andrew helped me to find a lot of the parts that I would not have found otherwise. He also did a lot of the physical work when my health was a little precarious. It was a good father and son project." Both Randy and Andrew posted questions and inquiries for parts in multiple Facebook groups, and soon those parts began arriving. The correct driveshaft was located in Arizona, a set of headliner bows came from a salvage yard in Pennsylvania, and a power brake booster arrived from Delaware. "Jim Drain in Clearwater, Florida is such a wealth of information! He also has a tremendous inventory of parts for the '66 and '67 Plymouth cars. I needed the guides and bushings for the right rear window. I called him, and a week later a package showed up." Of course, Randy and Andrew posted photos on social media regularly as the restoration progressed. Aficionados of the '67 GTX around the world followed their work.

There were two missing parts that proved troublesome. The first was the fold-down "buddy" seat which sits between the front bucket seats and fills the gap between them, making it possible for a third passenger to ride up front. After searching for a year, Rita discovered it at her father in-law's house. The other part, which has never turned up, was the fender tag, a two-inch by three-inch metal tag stamped with letters and numbers that correlate to the various accessories, paint codes, and interior trim codes from which a vehicle was assembled. Randy sent a letter to the Chrysler Historical Society, and they provided a copy of the IBM card that had been used by the factory when the car was built. By using the codes on the card as well as those on the assembly line build sheet, he was able to have the fender tag reproduced.

"When it went to the body shop, they media blasted it to remove the epoxy primer," Randy said. "They did the finish body work, and then they block sanded the whole car several times before painting it. They did a phenomenal job!"

No restoration is inexpensive, and costs add up quickly. "Before I started on this car, I was retired. But as the money started to run out, I had to go back to work in order to finish it. I couldn't stop half-way. My wife, Cheri, is okay with it, but we were looking forward to doing some traveling. This isn't how we had planned to spend our retirement years. I have every receipt for this car, but I'm afraid to add them up. I don't have enough nitroglycerine or enough Jack Daniels to do it."

The officials at the Muscle Car and Corvette Nationals, which is an annual show held in Chicago on the weekend before Thanksgiving, invited Randy to display it there upon completion. They were already familiar with his work and his high standards, for he had previously been invited to display his '71 Plymouth twice, and it had scored well in judging. "The MCACN show gave us a deadline," he said. Plagued by nagging health problems, however, the restoration took longer than anticipated. "We ended up taking the car to Keith Noel, who has a restoration shop in West Branch, Iowa. He installed the headliner, all of the glass, the seats, and he repainted the dashboard. When we got it back from him in October, we returned it to the body shop to have the paint wet sanded and buffed. The original windshield had a gouge from a worn-out wiper blade, but I had a guy come in and polish all of the glass. He was able to remove the gouge."

With the MCACN show now just a few weeks away, Randy and Andrew anxiously awaited the return of their grille and headlight bezels, which Jim Drain had sent out months earlier to be anodized and refinished. With less than a week to go, they got word that there had been a mistake made during the anodizing process, and all of the pieces had been damaged. "Jim Drain came to our rescue. He overnighted me new old stock (brand new original parts that had never been installed on a car) headlight bezels and a grille to use for the show. He lent them to me, and all I had to pay for was the overnight shipping." Andrew installed those pieces twelve hours before leaving for Chicago.

Randy, Cheri, and Andrew all headed to Chicago with the GTX strapped securely in their enclosed car trailer. Rita was to meet them there. They had all agreed ahead of time that she would install the last few pieces, thus completing the restoration. Before she arrived, Randy and Andrew parked the car in its assigned space in the convention center and they covered it. When Rita arrived, Randy uncovered the trunk lid and opened it. Rita installed the jack instruction sticker. Randy closed the trunk and covered it before moving to the driver's door jamb. There, Rita affixed the tire pressure sticker. Finally, they moved to the engine compartment where she installed the coolant sticker near the radiator. They did not allow her to see the whole car until she had completed it.

After Randy, Cheri, and Rita left the convention center for a rest, Andrew detailed the GTX. Randy said, "Andrew is absolutely the best detailer in the world. He is very finicky." A short while later, Andrew called Randy and said some judges were looking over the car. "I ran back over to the convention center. It was the first time I had ever seen my car set up for show. With Andrew's detail work, and sitting under the LED lights, it was like a scene from a movie where beams of light had come shining down from Heaven and illuminated it. I was flabbergasted! I started crying like a baby!"

Shortly after the Lowes arrived at the show, a beautiful red Road Runner convertible parked fifteen feet away. Randy said, "He had signs claiming that the car had over 200,000 miles on it, and a map showing where all it had been. He also had a story that had been published in Muscle Car Review about a road trip the owner had taken on Route 66. Jerry Shaw had ridden with him and documented the trip for the magazine story. Later, I introduced him to Rita, and they hit it off."

About the show, Rita said, "I had never experienced anything like it. People would come up and spend ten minutes looking at the car. There were lots of interesting people and so many beautiful cars! The Route 66 Road Runner was parked next to the GTX. Both articles about the trip had been written by Tom and photographed by Jerry. That was surreal! At the end of the show, Mopar Collectors Guide wanted to finish their photo shoot of the GTX. Randy asked me to ride with him to the wall where they wanted to photograph the car. I was thrilled, sitting the passenger's seat as I clutched my glass pendant with some of Jerry's ashes inside."

In judging, the Lowe family's efforts were rewarded with a score of 994 out of a possible 1000 points. Among the minor imperfections that detracted from their score were the hood pins. Although hood pins were available on certain models just a few years after the GTX had been built, they were not available on the '67 Plymouths. Randy explained, "Jerry had installed the hood pins. I knew they weren't factory-correct, but I decided to keep them as a nod toward him."

After the conclusion of the show, the cars were loaded into their various haulers and removed from the convention center. "The next morning, the place was empty except for a few semis," Randy said. "Cheri and I got into the GTX, and I took her for a ride around the inside of the building. Since we worked on it right up until the last minute, she had never ridden in it, and I had only driven it around our yard. But while we were driving around the convention center, my foot just <u>happened</u> to slip off the clutch, and, well, you know..." he chuckled. "Polyester tires on a polished concrete floor make a lot of noise! I didn't give it much gas, but it sure made its point. It was fun!"

Randy, Cheri, and Andrew plan to display their car at some of the bigger shows in the mid-west, but they also intend to make memories on the road with it. Randy said, "We have been invited back to MCACN next year, when the '67 model year will be featured." In the coming months, Rita will get her turn behind the wheel as well.

Two Continents and Half a Century in a '68 Shelby

Bill and Susan Stanley were high school sweethearts, and they began their life together as husband and wife shortly after their graduation. Not long afterward, Bill served a one-year tour of duty in Vietnam. When he returned home, he reenlisted in the Army, and he was stationed at Fort McClellan in Alabama. Being the car enthusiast that he was, he and Susan went to King Ford in nearby Anniston. Susan recalls that a part of the dealership was called the "snake pit," and that was where they kept the Shelby Mustangs. That was also where Bill spent his reenlistment bonus on a '68 Shelby Mustang GT 500 convertible.

Carroll Shelby was a racer who made a name for himself in the world of motorsports during the 1950s. At the close of the decade, after winning the 24 Hours of Le Mans, his driving career was curtailed by a heart condition. He started his own company, Shelby American, in 1962, and soon he was stuffing Ford V-8 engines into the tiny British built AC Ace chassis, which resulted in the AC Cobra. It was Shelby's intention to build a car that could dominate the Corvette on the racetrack. The AC Cobra soon morphed into the Shelby Cobra, and Shelby expanded his partnership with Ford Motor Company to include Mustangs that were modified in his shop and carried his name.

"We hadn't been married long, and I thought Bill wanted a Chevelle or a Corvette. I had never heard of a Shelby, and I was surprised when he bought it." For her, the Shelby was not love at first sight. "I was not happy!" Susan said. "He spent all of our money on that car." With a sticker price of 4,920 dollars, the Shelby was priced sixty percent higher than a base Mustang GT convertible. While the Shelby came at a significant premium over the standard Mustang, there was a comparable disparity in the driving experience. The Shelby version of the Mustang was equipped with a 428 cubic inch Police Interceptor engine, stiffer springs, a stiffer sway bar, front disc brakes, fifteen-inch wheels, and upgraded shock absorbers. It was also fitted with a fiberglass hood with integral scoops, a fiberglass lower valence, and a fiberglass trunk lid with an integrated spoiler, as well as a grille, taillights, and graphics specific to that model. For improved safety, all Shelbys came with a roll bar. "The first time I drove it, I fell in love with it! It was a Mustang on steroids."

Bill traded cars every few years, but when he talked of replacing the Shelby, Susan wouldn't hear of it. "I talked him into letting me take it over as my car, and then he could buy something else." Bill owned a succession of muscle cars including Pontiac Trans Ams and an AMC Javelin AMX, but it was the Shelby that stole Susan's heart. "I just couldn't bear to part with it."

Speaking about their early years with the Shelby, Susan said, "We moved around a lot as Bill was transferred from one place to another. We drove the Shelby across the country several times. It was a unique car, but it wasn't a special car back then. I have pictures of it covered with snow in Colorado. But right from the start, it looked different, and people always asked what it was. It was a conversation piece. I would come out of a store, and people would want to talk about it."

Soon, the Stanleys moved to Frankfurt, Germany for a year, and they took the Shelby with them. "Driving it on the Autobahn was quite an experience because there is no speed limit. Really, I was too young to have this car. I was only nineteen when I was driving it on the Autobahn."

When Bill and Susan returned to the 'States, they brought the Shelby back, and they continued driving it as their daily transportation. Although it was unique, Susan explained, "For the first ten years, it was just a car. As parts broke or wore out, they were replaced. That includes the carburetor."

Six years into his military career, Bill was diagnosed with diabetes, after which he was forced to retire. The couple then fell into a civilian lifestyle. "I had a forty-year career in banking," Susan said. Much of that time was spent at a bank in Paoli, Pennsylvania. "I drove the Shelby every day, and I parked it in the end space of the parking lot. Even now, people remember seeing it parked at the bank back then. The car was never garaged, but we had it repainted a couple of times, so it always looked pretty good. One summer, Bill and I sanded the whole car so my dad could repaint it."

Sadly, Bill passed away in 1997 due to complications of diabetes. "We were married for thirty years. His last two years were pretty rough. About two years after he passed, I saw a flyer for a car show and I decided to go. It was the first time I had smiled in a long time." After that, she became a regular car show attendee. "I would go to a car show on Saturday, maybe another one Saturday night, and then another one on Sunday."

As an introvert, Susan finds it difficult to make small talk with strangers. "I'm not really sure of myself. This car has helped me because it puts me out there. I'm nervous before a show, but this forces me to be more forward. If I'm with my car, I can talk to people."

In 2000, Susan turned her Shelby over to her brother, Stephen Capriola, for a restoration. Stephen owns Steve's Service in Malvern, Pennsylvania. Working on the Shelby between his customers' cars, the restoration took eight years to complete. She was delighted when the car was finished, but her elation was short lived. "I was involved in a traffic accident that damaged the front of the car. It's a memory I don't like, but it happened, and it is part of the car's history." The Shelby returned to Stephen's shop for two additional years' worth of repairs, and it has been lovingly cared for by Susan ever since. Although she retired it from daily use following its restoration, she said, "It's not trailered. I still drive it, but the shows I go to are mostly local." She added, "I like it when people recognize the car and tell me that they remember seeing it parked at the bank. It's nice to meet up with them again.

"Sometimes people ask me, how much is it worth? The car is special to me, and I can't put a price on it. I have a lot of memories, and I have had a lot of fun with it. It gave me something positive after my husband died. I am happy to have had it all these years, and I'm happy to represent Carroll Shelby. He seemed like a good man who liked people."

One of her greatest memories took place at the American Muscle Mustang Show in Media, Pennsylvania in 2015. Celebrity custom car builder Chip Foose selected it out of the 1500 cars present. In addition to winning a trophy, Foose made a drawing of her Shelby, and it was one of the vehicles selected for their 2016 calendar. As thrilled as she was, she said, "Everybody likes to win trophies, but that's not why I'm there. Car people are generally good people. I like them, and I like that they appreciate my car."

Susan said, "After fifteen years of being alone, I met a man named Joe Burke at a show, and we started going out. We have been together for almost ten years. People have gotten used to seeing his '55 Chevy Cameo truck and my Shelby pulling into shows together."

Few people keep a car for 54 years, but Susan's passion for her Shelby is just as strong today as it was the first time she drove it. Looking toward the future she said, "I'm 72 now, and I want to be happy." She plans to continue showing and enjoying her car.

Other titles from Higher Ground Books & Media:

Jack Kramer's Journey by Frank Adkins

Asleep at the Keyboard by Frank Adkins

Raven Transcending Fear by Terri Kozlowski

The Power of Knowing by Jean Walters

Forgiven and Not Forgotten by Terra Kern

Through the Sliver of a Frosted Window by Robin Melet

Breaking the Cycle by Willie Deeanjlo White

The Deception of 666 by Terra Kern

Chronicles of a Spiritual Journey by Stephen Shepherd

Eyes of Understanding by Stephen Shepherd

The Real Prison Diaries by Judy Frisby

Add these titles to your collection today!

http://www.highergroundbooksandmedia.com

HIGHER GROUND BOOKS & MEDIA IS

AN INDEPENDENT PUBLISHER

Do you have a story to tell?

Higher Ground Books & Media is an independent Christian-based publisher specializing in stories of triumph! Our purpose is to empower, inspire, and educate through the sharing of personal experiences. We are always looking for great, new stories to add to our collection. If you're looking for a publisher, get in touch with us today!

Please be sure to visit our website for our submission guidelines.

http://www.highergroundbooksandmedia.com/submission-guidelines

HGBM SERVICES IS OUR CONSULTING FIRM

AUTHOR SERVICES

HGBM Services offers a variety of writing and coaching services for aspiring authors! We can help with editing, manuscript critiques, self-publishing, and much more! Get in touch today to see how we can help you make your dream of becoming an author a reality!

*****

We also offer social media marketing services for authors, small businesses, and non-profit organizations. Let us help you get the word out about your book, your projects, and your mission. We offer great rates, quality promos, consistent communication, and a personal touch!

http://www.highergroundbooksandmedia.com/editing-writing-services

Need Bulk Copies?

If you would like to order bulk copies of this book or any other title at Higher Ground Books & Media, please contact us at highergroundbooksandmedia@gmail.com.

We offer discounts for purchases of 20 or more copies. Excellent for small groups, book clubs, classrooms, etc.

Get in touch today and get a set of great stories for your students or group members.